"DR. PICKARD'S JOURNEY to success as a multimillionaire and generous philanthropist was guided by the principles in *Surviving the Shift: 7 Proven Millionaire Moves for Embracing Change and Building Wealth*. Pickard survived and grew while others failed because he dreamed big, diversified his business, and formed profitable joint ventures and strategic partnerships. Pickard is truly a model for business aspirants all over the world."

—JAMES H. LOWRY, Senior Advisor for The Boston Consulting Group, Inaugural Member of the Minority Business Hall of Fame

"AN EXTRAORDINARY BOOK from a Super Extraordinary Human Being."

—CATHY HUGHES, Founder and Chairperson, TV One/Radio One, INC.

"I WAS FORTUNATE to work under Dr. Pickard's tutelage as an employee and later as a community leader. The wisdom and life lessons he shares are transformative."

—JUDGE GREG MATHIS, Warner Bros. Productions

"A MUST-READ for anyone interested in starting their own business or being successful working for corporate America."

—DENNIS W. ARCHER, Chairman & CEO of Dennis W. Archer PLLC, Mayor of Detroit (1994–2001)

"IF INSIGHT, WISDOM, and transformation from one of *Black Enterprise* magazine's 100 Top 10 Black businesses is your goal, I highly recommend that you sit at the feet of this master."

—GEORGE C. FRASER,
Ph.D., Speaker, Author, and Entrepreneur

"DR. PICKARD HAS BEEN a tremendous trailblazing entrepreneur. Most importantly, after reaching the summit of success, he has returned to the valley to guide and motivate future entrepreneurs to succeed. In this book, Dr. Pickard shows his consistency in looking, reaching, and giving back to those who will listen and learn. As you read this book you will experience Dr. Pickard's unique and piercing personality."

—ANTHONY C. NELSON, Ph.D., Dean,
School of Business, Professor,
Computer Information Systems,
North Carolina Central University

"BILL PICKARD'S GENEROSITY has impacted the lives of many people he has known and many more that he will never know, including students and alumni of Florida A&M University. His generosity exceeds far beyond financial support but includes sharing his wisdom and experiences that inspire students, faculty, and staff. His new book gives a firsthand account of a remarkable journey filled with nuggets that will motivate and guide us to help achieve our dreams."

—LARRY ROBINSON, Ph.D., President,
Florida A&M University (FAMU)

PRAISE for SURVIVING the SHIFT

"DR. WILLIAM PICKARD has a way of reaching across all age groups as he tells his engaging story of entrepreneurial success. I have watched as the School of Business and Industry (SBI) students delight in his humor and wisdom. They leave with a deeper understanding of what is necessary for long-term success in business and life. But more importantly, they leave with more drive and determination to succeed. *Surviving the Shift: 7 Proven Millionaire Moves for Embracing Change and Building Wealth* is a must-read for exploring the questions many of us are asking, 'What is this new normal, and how do we survive this shift to create the future of our dreams?'"

—**SHAWNTA FRIDAY-STROUD, Ph.D., Dean, School of Business and Industry, Vice President, University Advancement & Executive Director FAMU Foundation, Florida A&M University**

"AS A RESPECTED AND SUCCESSFUL entrepreneur, Dr. Pickard's book, *Surviving the Shift: 7 Proven Millionaire Moves for Embracing Change and Building Wealth,* will ensure future generations have a guidepost to exceptional business achievement. Dr. Pickard has proven that entrepreneurship and philanthropy can serve as mutual partners for the positive benefit of society. I am pleased that HBCUs will have this publication as a resource for their entrepreneurship programs.

—**DR. EVERETT B. WARD, Former President of St. Augustine's University and National President of Alpha Phi Alpha Fraternity**

"AFTER OVER THREE DECADES of friendship, I watched Bill Pickard grow yet never waver from his principles as he 'survived the shift.' He works hard, delivers excellence, and has built a foundation that with these principles will remain solid for decades to come."

—**TOMMY DORTCH, JR., Chairman and CEO of TWD, Inc., and National Chairman of 100 Black Men of America**

PRAISE for SURVIVING the SHIFT

"PICKARD'S CAREER as an entrepreneur and businessman is a true American story of success achieved through perseverance, determination, and a keen mind. His successes as a businessman and entrepreneur are matched by his passion and commitment to serve his community and to mentor young people. His book is a must-read for anyone who wishes to learn the lesson of how to do well while also doing good."

**—MARC H. MORIAL, President and CEO,
National Urban League**

"DR. BILL PICKARD'S thought-provoking wisdom helped shift my corporate mindset to entrepreneurship during our first encounter. Now, more than twenty-five years later, his prolific business advice, life lessons, and mentorship continue to be invaluable. Anyone in pursuit of the unconventional and determined to be successful despite failures should read Dr. Pickard's book *Surviving the Shift.*"

**—HIRAM E. JACKSON, Chief Executive Officer,
Real Times Media**

"I HAVE USED Dr. William Pickard's transferable entrepreneurial insights to run one of the most successful fraternal organizations in the USA."

**—MELVIN BAZEMORE, Esq., Lt. Grand Commander & COO,
United Supreme Council, Ancient Accepted Scottish Rite (PHA)**

"THIS BOOK IS SOMETHING we all have been waiting for…when you have a dedicated entrepreneur like Dr. Pickard who has always been willing to share not just his financial blessings but his wisdom, his positive attitude, his relationships, and his faith…you have everything that you need to be a success not just in business but also in life. I can bear witness that he is a man in love with his people and their achievement."

**—HARRY E. JOHNSON, Sr., President, Martin Luther King
National Memorial and Former President of Alpha Phi Alpha Fraternity**

PRAISE for SURVIVING the SHIFT

"AN INSIGHTFUL, MOTIVATING, illuminating, and instructional guide to entrepreneurship, a must-read if you ever want to achieve success in today's business environment. Having personally witnessed Dr. Pickard's triumphs in business and been counseled firsthand by his wisdom, I am confident that the insights in *Surviving the Shift: 7 Proven Millionaire Moves for Embracing Change and Building Wealth* can help hardworking entrepreneurs become prosperous business owners."

—TONI RODGERS,
McDonald's Franchise Owner and Entrepreneur

"THIS BOOK IS ENTERTAINING and full of metaphors and engaging stories that provide a window into Dr. Pickard's world of proven and practical insights, methods, and tools. As the past dean of a college of business, I have seen first-hand how his pragmatic approach to business ownership adds value to classroom discussions and provides immediately actionable advice to seasoned entrepreneurs."

—DR. LE-QUITA BOOTH, Former Dean
of Alabama State University School of Business

"*SURVIVING THE SHIFT: 7 Proven Millionaire Moves for Embracing Change and Building Wealth* is a life-changing, inspiring, and thought-provoking masterpiece that is profoundly insightful and electrifying. It is a must-read for all entrepreneurs and aspiring entrepreneurs who aspire to reach the pinnacle of business success."

—DR. MILLICENT LOWNES-JACKSON, Dean,
The College of Business, Tennessee State University

PRAISE for SURVIVING the SHIFT

"BILL PICKARD is a self-made entrepreneur who has not only survived in business but has thrived over fifty years. The principles that he outlines in his book, *Surviving the Shift: 7 Proven Millionaire Moves for Embracing Change and Building Wealth,* can serve as a blueprint for young entrepreneurs around the world."

— **LECESTER (BILL) ALLEN, Founder and President of the Allen Entrepreneurial Institute International (AEII) at Camp Exposure**

"*SURVIVING THE SHIFT: 7 Proven Millionaire Moves for Embracing Change and Building Wealth* by Dr. William F. Pickard is a delightful overview on the way we do business in the twenty-first century. He writes with humor that cleverly and explosively makes you laugh, cry, feel encouraged, probably even get mad and, most importantly, think. Read this book at the risk of causing a positive change in your life or business. A must-read for all entrepreneurs or those aspiring to be an entrepreneur."

— **ANTHONY NEGBENEBOR, Ph.D., Dean Emeritus and Dover Chair of Business, Gardner-Webb University, Past President, Accreditation Council for Business Schools and Programs (ACBSP)**

"THIS BOOK ABSOLUTELY captures the essence of one of our most distinguished Black business leaders and does it in a way that is highly instructive for both aspiring and experienced entrepreneurs alike. Not only is Dr. Pickard's personal journey inspiring, but he also gives his readers the gift of a proven road map that reveals the optimal path to success in any operating environment."

— **SONYA S. MAYS, President and CEO, Develop Detroit**

PRAISE for SURVIVING the SHIFT

"DR. PICKARD SHARES the principles that propelled his meteoric success in a very pragmatic, understandable, and actionable way. His personal example of taking a holistic approach to business success is appropriately steeped in personal commitment, growth, intentionality, hard work, and faith. *Surviving the Shift: 7 Proven Millionaire Moves for Embracing Change and Building Wealth* is a must-read primer, guide, and resource not only for business success but for success in life!"

—JEROME HUTCHINSON, JR., Founder & Chief Servant Officer, ICABA-International Career and Business Alliance, Inc.

"DR. PICKARD'S ENGAGING and illuminating narrative speaks to the best in us all. I think his seven principles are essential fertilizer for young minds seeking to overcome fear and negativity. Blessed with the ability to deftly navigate class and culture Pickard draws the reader in with both empathy and inspiration. As an artist and educator in Harlem in NYC, I see the immense worth of voices like Dr. Pickard's as the next generation ripens."

—M. SCOTT JOHNSON, Internationally Renowned Sculptor and Educator at the Schomburg Center for Research in Black Culture

"DR. BILL PICKARD gives the best tools for business success all in one place. I watched Bill survive the shift! This is the action guide you will never be without as you move through business, academics, and life. Embracing change and building wealth are your expected results."

—DR. GEORGE T. FRENCH, President, Clark Atlanta University

SURVIVING
THE SHIFT

SURVIVING
THE SHIFT

PROVEN
MILLIONAIRE
MOVES

FOR EMBRACING
CHANGE AND
BUILDING WEALTH

WILLIAM F. PICKARD, PhD

Forefront
BOOKS

Published by Forefront Books.
Distributed by Simon & Schuster.

Library of Congress Control Number: 2022914878

Print ISBN: 978-1-94867-778-3
E-book ISBN: 978-1-94867-779-0

Cover Design by Bruce Gore, GORE STUDIO, INC.
Interior Design by Mary Susan Oleson, BLU DESIGN CONCEPTS

TABLE *of* CONTENTS

Foreword

"LIFE'S GREATEST TRAGEDY is to already be where you are going" sermonically suggested my late mentor, Reverend Manuel L. Scott, Sr. This proverb by one of the princes of the pulpit is a warning against becoming "stuck like Chuck" and reducing one's sense of possibility to current circumstances. Life is dynamic, ever beckoning us to become more than we are; however, many people lead static lives, going where they've been, doing what they have done, and living life on "repeat," especially with their finances and their career. Mufasa, in the Disney animated classic movie *The Lion King*, remixes Scott and indicts Simba, "Simba, you have forgotten me. You are more than what you have become." Simba was living beneath his potential, squandering his life, stuck in sameness, because the tragedy that had befallen him had gotten to him and in him, and reduced his sense of possibility. Simba, as are so many like the would-be "Lion King," needed the life lessons William F. Pickard provides for us in *Surviving the Shift: 7 Proven Millionaire Moves for Embracing Change and Building Wealth*.

This book can liberate you from the tragedy of already

being where you are going and take you on an empowering journey to wealth, wholeness, and "living your best life" while doing good in the world.

Bill has a powerful testimony, and in these pages, he takes the "witness stand" and brilliantly shares the lessons he has learned, even from the school of hard knocks. The proven principles in *Surviving the Shift* provide the reader with an empowering, entrepreneurial, and economic "GPS" so that you can make moves from where you are to the "abundant life." Bill has successfully taken the journey and overcome odds and racial injustice while being committed to opening doors of opportunity for others. He has done well, and he is committed to "spreading the wealth." Bill could say of himself what Jay-Z says when he raps "I went from pauper to president, cause every deal ever made set precedent." He is a game-changing exemplar who has made moves that provide for all of us instruction and motivation. Read this "GPS" and start making moves to your best life.

You will enjoy and be enlightened by *Surviving the Shift* as you experience the energy and scintillating personality of Bill leaping from the pages. It was said of Jesus in the gospels that "the common people heard him gladly" and that He "spoke with authority, not like the scribes and Pharisees." Bill has that linguistic flavor in *Surviving the Shift*. On the same page, he can make you laugh and quote hip-hop artists and the "numbers man," while "dropping knowledge" that is transformational. He knows the language of the streets and he is conversant with those in corporate and political suites. "Everyday people" will read this "gladly" and know that the brotha knows what he's talking about. He's got the receipts! This "GPS" will provide you with direction and you will be fueled by the vim and voice of the author.

It must be noted that *Surviving the Shift* is not a shallow, cheerleading motivational book that ignores the crushing realities of oppression and injustice that limit opportunities and are set to preclude one's possibilities. During a recent television commercial about the YMCA, the narrator said, "In America, the zip code you grow up in can determine your future, your school, your job, your dreams, your problems." Sadly, many are born into conditions that undermine potential and add to the wealth and achievement gaps. However, Bill, who was born in a zip code designed by oppression to limit what he could become, broke through barriers and overcame the "zip code odds." He understands the pain of zip code injustice, but he provides insights for overcoming. Bill transformed the adversity he has experienced into a university that educated, stretched, and gave him an undeniable sense of what can be. As Bill says about himself, he is a visionary.

There is a camera phone that is advertised as having what is called "night sight." The darkness of night doesn't prohibit it from capturing and providing beautiful pictures. Bill, in these pages, has provided the reader with "night sight." We are living in dark times, but the night sight of Bill Pickard will help you to see your way to a blessed and successful life. You don't have to spend the rest of your life with the limitations that come with signing the back of your check. Are you ready to create the entrepreneurial picture of a new life? Read and follow the instructions of this GPS and start making millionaire moves.

—Frederick Douglass Haynes, III

Introduction

I FULLY EMBRACE THE MANTRA "Each one, reach one, teach one." These words get me fired up. They also explain the purpose of this book. This is my way of giving back, and it's my way of saying that whatever I've done, you can do it too. It doesn't matter who you are—a blue-collar worker, an MBA grad, a new business owner, or a student working nights to pay your way through school.

If you're reading this, I suspect you are ready to do more than talk a good game. No doubt, you're tired of waiting, hoping, and dreaming. You're eager to lace up your track shoes and sprint all the way to the Fortune 500 finish line.

My brother, my sister, I feel you. I know about the challenges. I recognize your frustrations and the dozens of tasks you're juggling. As an up-and-coming entrepreneur, chances are you're trying to identify the right employees, organize your schedule, and find a mentor or confidante—anyone to offer guidance. If you're wise, you're checking out a number of finance options and taking some extra precautions to build your reputation, stabilize your credit, and save.

Consider *Surviving the Shift* an essential part of that effort. I've packed a lot of advice into these pages, and I believe the insights you gain will give you what you need to turn your hustle into a thriving enterprise. Don't get me wrong; I know nothing is foolproof. However, I'm convinced the tools presented here will help you jump over the next hurdle. Why? Because they did that for me.

I've been where you probably are right now. Whether you're riding the tide of a financial windfall, struggling to pass an economic theory class, or praying to keep your fledgling operation in the black—yep, I've experienced it too. I've dealt with the smackdowns, and I've struggled to overcome doubt. But I've also known the surge of unbeatable confidence. In the end, I conquered. I beat the odds. I soared.

That's what distinguishes my message and sets *Surviving the Shift* apart from the rest. There is a surplus of inspirational, how-to-be-a-winner books on the market, and they all claim to have the answers. But the one you're holding in your hands right now was written by someone who knows the proverbial ropes and has taken the risks. I have the balance sheet and net worth to prove it.

I'm the chairman of Global Automotive Alliance, one of the country's leading minority-owned companies and the first minority-owned group of tier-one and tier-two suppliers of plastic parts to the top three automakers in the United States. By 2014, we had sales of $475 million. Meanwhile, I've been able to hire individuals looking for their first big break and establish internship programs to recruit the next generation of minority employees in plastics processing.

But none of this happened overnight. As someone who has been on his own payroll since the age of twenty-eight, I'm the first to admit it's been a long trek, one that included more than a few frantic days and sleepless nights. It would have been really easy to give up. I had plans to be a social worker, and it would have been much more comfortable for me to do just that—settle for a college degree and a nine-to-five job.

Instead, I chose the path of self-reliance. Of course, that meant I had to deal with my share of skeptics, cynics, and racists. I kept going anyway. The way I see it, haters are just another part of the experience. If you're a person of color, some form of prejudice is going to try to trip you up sooner or later. It's up to you to maneuver around it, under it, over it, or through it. That's never been more difficult than after a world-wide pandemic, but I'm here to tell you that you can do it.

In *Surviving the Shift*, I have chosen not to dwell on forecasts of discrimination. To explain why, I have to reflect on something I learned from Walter Douglas, the former head of New Detroit, a coalition of civil rights and social justice leaders. During a meeting back in the 1980s, someone asked Douglas about the difficulties minorities faced securing business contracts. His response was priceless.

"Racism is like the weather," he said. "On some days you need your overcoat, your scarf, your hat, mittens, and snow boots. Then, there are days when you simply need a heavy sweater or a trench coat."

So when something or someone tries to block you, button up your jacket and hold tight to your convictions. That's always been the way I roll. I told myself I could do it—and I did. With the exception of a college teaching stint and four combined years working for the Urban League and the NAACP, I have never really considered myself an employee. I became an *employer* fifty years ago—and I haven't looked back.

Actually, let me correct that statement. I look back occasionally, but when I do, I'm reminding myself of lessons learned and using those lessons to encourage those who are following a similar path. Those who are choosing independence. Those free-spirited upstarts such as you. I'm a visionary who believes in the potential of anyone with a positive attitude and a great idea. My goal is to show you how to transform that idea into a profitable endeavor.

Are you ready to make it happen? Then turn the page.

—William F. Pickard, PhD

CHAPTER 1

My Road to Success

It would be fair to say I was kind of tense that brisk autumn evening. I was the special guest at an annual dinner filled with news reporters, and I wasn't quite sure what to expect. All around me, cameras were flashing. And people I didn't even know were praising me and shaking my hand.

After smiling politely and engaging in the usual social banter, I slipped into a seat behind the dais and waited for the program to begin. When it finally started, I felt that charge I always get. You know, that art-of-the-deal adrenaline? I was pumped up, ready to talk business.

But that was not why we were here. Instead, I was regaled with a running list of my achievements. I heard about my life, my contributions, and all the hurdles I had leaped. And there, before an audience of journalists, civic leaders, and elected officials, I was given one of the highest honors of the state—The Detroit News 2001 Michiganians of the Year Award, a recognition based on "good works" Detroit citizens have done to elevate the community.

I was elated and, at the same time, still a bit unnerved. For one thing, I prefer being behind the scenes. For another, well, let's just say I didn't quite see myself in the same category as some of the past recipients—internationally known Michiganians such as Rosa Parks, Lee Iacocca, and Aretha Franklin. They were celebrities, but I still saw myself as just a chubby kid from a small town in Georgia. Although I'd become a multinational CEO with a portfolio of major enterprises, I was still coming to terms with my rise from humble beginnings. In the years preceding the Michiganians of the Year distinction, I had earned a bachelor of arts, a master's degree in social work, and a doctorate, all the while fending off doubts from those around me.

No one expected me to graduate from college. After all, I was awkward and could barely see without my glasses. I had no idea that, one day, I'd own McDonald's franchises, become comanaging partner of the MGM Detroit Casino, or become the co-owner of five Black-owned newspapers. Who could have predicted that I would establish an automotive alliance with eight manufacturing plants in the United States and Canada? And who knew that I'd ever be under such a prestigious spotlight, being fêted by some of Detroit's finest dignitaries?

As the applause thundered, I overcame my momentary insecurity, stood up proudly, and gazed out at the crowd. Some of my friends were there—federal judge Damon J.

Keith, Mayor Dennis Wayne Archer, and Arthur and Chacona Johnson—along with my (now-ex) wife, Vivian Rogers Pickard, and many noteworthy individuals I had just met. I looked at them all with a sense of gratitude and respect. These were not the kind of men and women I had encountered in my childhood circle of blue-collar employees, struggling day laborers, hustlers, "numbers men," and slickly dressed gamblers.

But, as the saying goes, life can change on a dime. This fickle thing we call "everyday living" is chock-full of haphazard twists, poetic ironies, and subtle, hairpin turns. It doesn't matter where you begin. If you work hard enough, the most unfavorable circumstances can become a landslide of sweet victories. All it takes is drive, teamwork, and plain old-fashioned stick-to-itiveness.

In a nutshell, that's the basis of my success, and it's the basis of the lessons you're about to explore. Consider this book a comprehensive guide to self-determination, entrepreneurship, and business leadership, replete with instructions on how to dodge the land mines you'll run into along the way. There's no such thing as a shortcut to success. You're either in it to win it and prepared to do whatever it takes, or you're a pushover, the type who runs away when too many obstacles surface and the road that sprawls ahead is covered with barbed wire and broken glass. If you've been the latter, then I suggest one of two things: either put this book down and abandon your dream . . . or dig in your heels and make a vow that nothing will ever stand between you and the promised land.

The chapters that follow are going to show you how to keep that vow. After reading them, you'll know how to tap inner resources you probably didn't know existed. Further, you will have a dynamic business methodology on how to:

- establish a reliable network.
- maintain a high level of liquidity.
- develop multiple income streams.
- build sustainable wealth.

You also will learn about something I was lucky enough to inherit: common sense. Yes, it's true. Common sense, that so-called basic instinct, is as important as education, flowcharts, and spreadsheets. Thankfully, it landed in my lap at a young age, compliments of my dear old, streetwise, fast-talking Uncle Paul. Now, I'm not saying Uncle Paul was a business genius or that the lessons he imparted were the cornerstone of my achievements. However, I readily acknowledge that his savvy, gut-level insights have had a major impact on my life.

For that reason, I'm passing them on. I'm singing the praises and exposing the strategies of a man known about town for his unbeatable confidence, macho swagger, and a pocket that was always stuffed with money. He was a "numbers man" and, in the 1950s and 1960s, it was no secret how much that meant in the Black community. I got to know him after my parents (Dad worked in the auto plant and Mama was a day worker) moved our family from LaGrange, Georgia, to Flint, Michigan. Eventually we settled into a lower middle-income neighborhood with a sprinkling of Black businesses, including a record shop owned by Flint boxing legend Larry Watkins.

Larry gave me my first job and exposed me to business techniques that would serve me well later in life. Under his wing, I learned customer relations and the importance of cash flow. Larry also had a unique way of promoting his business. Every Sunday he played nothing but gospel music, and, sure enough, the church folks would pile into the store and buy albums featuring James Cleveland, The Soul Stirrers, and others. In those days, we didn't use the term *strategic marketing*, but that's exactly what Larry was doing. Although I didn't realize it at the time, he and Uncle Paul were my first real entrepreneurial role models.

Since those years, I've met and been inspired by many high-profile leaders—from Malcolm X to Henry Ford—but when I teach business seminars at colleges around the country, I usually offer this anecdote:

In 1955, a young Black man graduates from the Meharry Medical College School of Dentistry, and he's number one in his class. He returns to Detroit and wants to open his dental practice. He needs an office manager, he needs some money, and he needs equipment, and it all comes to $4,500. Where does the money come from?

Inevitably, a few students will answer, "He goes to the bank." Others will shout out, "His family has money." Then I always look at the class and smile.

"No," I reply. "In many cases, his daddy went to the numbers man, and the numbers man loaned him the money.

That was our economy. That was our bank. As a rule, in 1955, very few banks would loan a Black man money to open a business."

Next I tell the class that I could introduce them to undertakers who successfully operated funeral homes for thirty years but still could not get a bank loan. They, too, were financed by the numbers man. Uncle Paul not only taught me this but also showed me with his own clever, cool example and a litany of tips. Among them:

"Never try to hustle a hustler."

"Always give the sucker another break."

Those sayings would be most instructive to me later in life, especially when I invested in my first McDonald's franchise.

My favorite?

"Always leave something on the table for the sucker. That way, he'll always come back."

In other words, we're part of an ecosystem. Just as farmers leave corn in the fields to attract deer and other animals to protect their crops, Uncle Paul realized that he needed to ensure that individuals who patronized his establishments returned again and again.

This suggestion intrigued me, and—like most of the advice I gained from Uncle Paul—it's left an indelible mark on my mind. I've filed his lessons up there with the best of them—the ones I learned at universities and the ones gained in the proverbial School of Hard Knocks.

Yes, I've learned from my successes. But I've learned even more from my failures.

That, perhaps, is one of the most important messages you will glean from my experiences. You'll discover that a rare few people will travel a road that is smoothly paved all the way from the beginning to the end. On your way to business leadership, you'll discover it's OK to stumble in the process of getting where you want to go. Mistakes happen. In fact, it's a guarantee at some point.

The only people who don't mess up are the ones who don't try. It's like that with anything you attempt: a jump shot on the basketball court, a rigorous triathlon, or something as simple as skateboarding down the road. People who skateboard often get a few scratches and scrapes on their arms and legs. If they don't tumble a few times, that means they didn't attempt any daring new hops or tricks. They simply played it safe and rolled down the road.

That's not what successful people are aiming for, and neither should you.

If you're serious about becoming an entrepreneur, you're not interested in circling the same route over and over. You're shooting for a higher, faster track, which means you need to take calculated risks. Risk-takers are the ones who move beyond their staid, rank-and-file job and find a way to jump-start their fortune.

For me, that jump-start was a McDonald's franchise. My two partners, Raymond Snowden and Melvin Garrett, and I were among the first African Americans to own a "Mickey D's" in the United States. But like most of my accomplishments, it couldn't have happened without discipline and a strict adherence to my cherished rules. I call them my Seven Proven Principles of Entrepreneurship:

1. Develop positive *vision* and *attitude*. They represent foresight and the ability to sustain an image of something that has not yet manifested.

2. Be mindful of *opportunity*. Always search for what's missing and fill the void with ideas and actions.

3. Look for *finance* options everywhere, starting with your own personal savings account.

4. Build good *relationships*. They are worth their weight in diamonds.

5. Choose a team with the right *talent* and *skill set*. They are the foundation of a business.

6. Do not overreact to *failure*. It's like gravity. Sometimes you fall. But if you do, all you have to do is get up again.

7. Cultivate strong *faith*. It's the fuse that electrifies my soul, creates new goals, and expands dreams.

These are the keystones that fired up my spirit and enabled me to pursue my first real venture. They are the guidelines I developed and nurtured over the years as I invested in myriad enterprises, juggled various businesses, and established multiple streams of income. I have grown along the way and so has my entrepreneurial acumen. Yet I have never stopped believing in and cultivating these seven principles.

Who knows where I would be if I hadn't followed them when I took on what I now consider one of the most significant positions of my early career? The year was 1967, and I was a twenty-seven-year-old social worker serving as executive director for the Cleveland branch of the NAACP. The organization was calling for change and leading a boycott against Carling Black Label beer. A brewery and distribution center in the heart of the Black community, Carling was a supplier for Black bars and restaurants. However, it hired very few Black employees and had no Black delivery truck drivers. The NAACP leadership began meeting with Carling representatives daily.

Meanwhile, my boss and a group of investors brokered an under-the-table deal to become owners of the Carling distributorship in Cleveland. I was shocked. My boss had not considered how the community would be affected by his personal deal, nor had he thought about me. This was my first wake-up call about leadership, politics, and the importance of securing a seat at the bargaining table. It taught me about trust. It showed me that people, even those promoting causes, can be self-serving. And it inspired me to always seize the moment.

Ironically, this strange chain of events would change my life.

At the time, there was a street hustler (who will remain unnamed) in the Black community who was making so much noise about injustice that people began to regard him as an activist. He was outspoken, fiery, and, according to some, had questionable motives. Clearly, he was a force to be reckoned with. He led a group of Black Nationalists, and they were some *baaad* brothers. Whenever they placed that red, black, and green liberation flag in front of a restaurant, business would drop by at least 80 percent.

It wasn't long before McDonald's became their target. When the Black Nationalists discovered that not a single Black person had ever owned a McDonald's franchise in the United States, they launched what became known as Operation Black Unity. Of course, this attracted the attention of my NAACP boss, and we both sprang into action. The circumstances that followed exploded into one of the most successful economic boycotts in the history of the civil rights movement and became a pivotal part of my journey to financial independence.

Throughout the boycott, I maintained the *vision* and belief in the possibility of a Black franchise owner (Principle 1); worked diligently and took advantage of *opportunities* (Principle 2); understood the importance of *finance* (Principle 3); developed *relationships* (Principle 4); sought out *talent* (Principle 5); prepared for *failure* (Principle 6); and had unswerving *faith* (Principle 7) in things working out for the higher good of our community.

So several years later, when I received a call from the McDonald's regional office in Columbus, Ohio, I wasn't totally surprised. And I wasn't afraid of the challenge, especially since the US Small Business Administration was guaranteeing 75 percent of the loan. Because I was working on my doctorate at the time, I took out a loan for my portion of the down payment and Ray Snowden and Melvin Garrett, my friends and franchise business partners, came up with the rest—a total of $25,000 in equity.

Now, some people might be tempted to describe this situation as a dash of luck and a touch of providence. Others might use labels such as destiny and fate. I have another way of looking at it. I perceive luck as something that happens when preparation collides with opportunity. I reject the notion that our lives are ruled by an unyielding force called destiny, and I never take a fatalistic approach to anything.

What I do believe in is laying the groundwork, staying the course, and blazing trails for those who will one day fill my shoes. I'm bragging a little bit, but my company did almost a half-billion dollars in sales in 2015 and landed in the number eight spot on *Black Enterprise*'s Top 100 Black Businesses list (the BE#100s). I employ nearly three thousand people, and a lot of them look like me.

In the chapters that follow, you will find a breakdown of my Seven Proven Principles. No, they are not easy. And no, they are not going to reward you with instant wealth. But if you thoroughly study them and apply them accordingly, I'm sure you'll find them as indispensable as I do. They will mold you and help you stay afloat in the rough-and-tumble world of free enterprise.

They will serve as your road map—both now and for many years to come.

CHAPTER 2

PRINCIPLE 1:
Develop Positive Vision and Attitude

*You can never cross the ocean until you have
the courage to lose sight of the shore.*
—Anonymous

SHE SCRUBBED CLOTHES ALL DAY LONG and sometimes half the night. Still, the young washerwoman—a former sharecropper from the Louisiana Delta—barely earned enough to make ends meet. She was a recent widow, so broke and stressed that her hair was falling out. Her scalp itched something fearsome, and every time she scratched, it bled. She coped by smearing it with a peculiar-smelling ointment, handmade from her own secret ingredients.

Thus began the powerful mission of Madam C. J. Walker, the nation's first Black female millionaire. Many people have probably heard her rags-to-riches story, and many are aware of the national beauty company she built in the early 1900s, Madam C. J. Walker Manufacturing Company. But not everyone knows that it took more than long hours, tireless work—and the invention of a straightening comb—to catapult her to success. Her extraordinary achievements were rooted in her indomitable spirit and a concept that many take for granted. It's called *vision*.

THE YIN AND YANG OF YOUR SUCCESS

Vision is foresight and the ability to sustain an image of something that has not yet manifested. It's the two-hundred-unit apartment tower you expect to develop. It's the chain of neighborhood laundromats you sometimes daydream about. It's the business that grosses $100 million annually and maintains a global clientele. It's the thing you focus on with the intention of bringing it into existence.

You have to be able to see the perfect credit score; you have to picture yourself walking into the bank and depositing that seven-figure check. You absolutely have to believe it and keep your thoughts aligned with your goal. For instance, I can ask one person, "How are you doing today?" and hear back, "I'm alright," versus another person's response, "It's a great day! I'm glad to be up. I'm going to make something happen!"

That's where attitude comes into play. Vision and attitude are like yin and yang. The vision you are holding is based on the attitude you have been nourishing. Attitude is the emotion that gives birth to your desires and propels you forward. It's the perspective that fuels your imagination and enables you to see things today that will transform your business tomorrow. When you become a visionary, you learn to adjust your lens and shift your perceptions, especially the images you have of yourself.

I know this firsthand. In high school, I didn't consider myself a scholar and never excelled in sports. I used to hang out with the "losers" club that ate lunch under the staircase and did just enough homework to get by. Luckily for me, one of my teachers, Helen Steele, decided to push me beyond my self-imposed boundaries. She approached me one day after English class and spoke to me quite bluntly.

"You have a good mind," she said. "Why don't you use it?"

At first, I was baffled. *A good mind?* Me? I thought she had lost it. Yet a little voice deep inside of me toyed with the idea that she might actually be right. Her words sort of hovered and danced around my spirit. I delighted in flipping through my textbooks after that, and I read them with a little more zeal. I even started to walk differently. I don't know if I ever told Ms. Steele this, but her statement shook me out of my complacency and marked a turning point in my academic years. I became more assertive. My curiosity was piqued, and before long, Ms. Steele's accusatory question became the seed for a new and positive self-image. My doubts had waned, and I was beginning to see beyond my narrow parameters.

Hip-hop artist and business mogul Jay-Z put it this way:

"Your vision must be greater than the window you're looking through."[1]

Now, that's profound when you think about it. It sums up my situation as a youth and captures the plight of so many young men of color. A young man staring out of a small, obstructed window in Brooklyn's Marcy Projects probably can't see much with his eyes, but his mind can help him peer around the corner, across the bridge, and into the future.

And so it was with Madam C. J. Walker. Others may have viewed her as a poor, uneducated woman of color. But that's not the way she viewed herself. She imagined wealth, luxury, exquisite garments. She pushed her immediate circumstances out of her mind and refused to dwell on the pain of her past. She looked ahead instead of looking back.

To keep her thoughts flowing in the right direction, Madam Walker knew she needed support. So she found a piece of plywood and covered it with pictures she'd cut out of a Sears, Roebuck and Co. catalog. She nailed the wood, which she called her "wish board," to the wall of the bedroom she shared with her eleven-year-old daughter, Lelia. Each night, she and Lelia would glance at the images before falling asleep. They'd see them again in the morning as they dressed.

This practice is known today as creative visualization, and poster boards, vaguely similar to the wooden one used by Madam Walker, are all the rage. These days, they've been dubbed "vision boards," which is a trendy buzzword for a personal montage of photos, affirmations, and magazine clippings that reflect an individual's greatest aspirations. It's an effective tool for training the mind and keeping it riveted on ultimate victory.

TV game show host and actor Steve Harvey is a big believer in vision boards. In fact, he once told a live audience at a taping of *Family Feud* that "if you do not have it written down, your chances of it happening is reduced drastically because it's a principle of success. You have to have everything you want written."[2] Harvey even noted that the Bible tells us to do it:

Write down the revelation and make it plain on tablets so that a herald may run with it. For the revelation awaits an appointed time; it speaks of the end and will not prove false. Though it linger, wait for it; it will certainly come and will not delay. (Habakkuk 2:2–4 NIV)

Harvey visualizes everything he wants and writes it down. He has even gone as far as having his tailor embroider the number 3.5 on his shirts, suit jackets, and pants. That number represents 3.5 million, the TV rating he needs for his shows to succeed.

Media mogul Oprah Winfrey is the person who inspired Harvey to use vision boards. She had never used one until she heard Michelle Obama say something at a political rally in California in 2008. "At the end of the rally Michelle Obama said something powerful, 'and I want you to leave here and envision Barack Obama taking the oath of office.'"[3] Oprah went home and made a vision board, which included a photograph of the gown she would wear to President Obama's inauguration. She had the gown made and wore the stunning black dress to the historic event in Washington, DC, in January 2009.

Though she was new to vision boards, Oprah knew a lot about turning vision into reality. Before she became one of the most famous women in the world, she had to pull herself out of poverty. As a child watching her grandmother work tirelessly for very little, she told herself over and over again, *My life won't be like this. My life won't be like this, it will be better.*[4] And it was.

Of course, the creative visualization or the visioning process doesn't begin or end with this technique. Successful people have admitted that they often take time out of their busy schedules just to kick back in their offices, cars, or homes, imagining themselves in a more exciting setting. In fact, I've done this myself. Years ago, my business partners and I opened a McDonald's in Detroit on Woodward Avenue, one of the longest and busiest streets in the city. I still remember that moment, even though I wasn't experiencing the thrill in the same manner as everyone else. While the aroma of burgers wafted through the restaurant and my business cohorts were giving each other high-fives, I was flirting with images of our next venture. I was happy our first business was a success because I knew so many others failed. I wasn't taking anything for granted, but I was already setting my mind on the next big thing. Physically I was under the golden arches on Woodward, but in my mind I was scouting out a new site in neighboring Highland Park and picturing yet another one on Eight Mile Road. Eventually, those sites and more materialized—nine to be exact. But even at that point, I was already contemplating another future project.

It's not that I wasn't interested in being in the moment.

I'm just not the kind of person who gets stuck on the main attraction. In my head, I've already moved on. And why not? If I never *see* anything else, then there will never *be* anything else. This is the chief reason a number of companies are incorporating creative visualization sessions into their leadership and management workshops. It's a method of prodding their employees to reach higher and be more productive. It forces them out of their comfort zones and creates a template for growth.

Like vision boards, creative visualization—which I like to think of as vision that's so hot it's on fire—is as foolproof as gravity and other scientific laws. This method works so well that even Olympic athletes are trying it. They practice incessantly, but they also spend fifteen to twenty minutes, three or more times a week, picturing themselves performing the feat they expect to master. The same is true for US Navy SEALs. To survive as a Navy SEAL, one must be able to remain calm during episodes of intense terror. These warriors endure a rigorous, backbreaking boot camp and deprivation that would make the average person faint. But one of the critical components of their mental toughness training includes visualization strategies.

Let's stop and mull that over for a minute. Am I implying that you should spend valuable time rearranging the familiar pictures that have settled in your mind? The answer is an unequivocal *yes*. The brain is a source of power, and that power is deeper and far more expansive than simply memorizing facts and adding up numerical figures. Business sense doesn't end with your management skills and your ability to organize a successful financial campaign or PowerPoint presentation.

As Albert Einstein once explained, "Imagination is far more important than knowledge. Knowledge is limited to all we now know and understand, while imagination embraces the entire world and all there ever will be to know and understand."[5]

But how do you get there? How do you focus your mind to create a perfect vision of where you want to go? I have eleven tips that will help you get into this visionary frame of mind, and we'll spend the rest of this chapter unpacking them.

VISION TIP #1:
DRAW STRENGTH FROM YOUR SQUAD

Make your friends your brain trust. Bouncing and vibing off one another create a synergy. Henry Ford, Harvey Firestone, and Thomas Edison knew this and used it to their advantage. When they came together, ideas flowed freely and the magic of their collective genius was ignited. Authors C. S. Lewis, J. R. R. Tolkien, and Owen Barfield had a similar relationship in a group they dubbed the Inklings. Think of King Arthur and the Knights of the Round Table. Former Detroit mayor Dennis W. Archer; Ronald E. Hall, CEO of Bridgewater Interiors; Roy S. Roberts, group vice president of General Motors; and I shared a similar bond, and it contributed to our combined success.

In some circles, this "squad approach" is known as *masterminding*. Individuals in mastermind groups get together and hold the vision for each other. They discuss one's highest hopes, and each of them encourages the other to recalibrate their thoughts and take them to the next level.

VISION TIP #2:
FANTASIZE

If you're only thinking about what is *currently* going on in your life, you're already out of focus. Don't allow reality to completely dictate your perspective. Every now and then, forget about the roadblocks that surround you and simply imagine what you want. Seriously, try it. For this exercise, you don't have to close your eyes, but you must ignore images of what's annoying you and replace them with vibrant scenes of what you desire. If you can, try to add some emotion. Feel the joy and enthusiasm of landing that promotion or finalizing that multimillion-dollar deal.

You'd be surprised at how many famous and successful people do this. Before Jim Carrey was one of the biggest stars in Hollywood, he was a struggling actor who was barely getting by. As motivation, Carrey wrote himself a check for ten million dollars and put it in his wallet. In 1994, a movie studio wrote him a ten-million-dollar check to star in *Dumb and Dumber*.[6] Similarly, when the New England Patriots failed to reach the Super Bowl in 2016, quarterback Tom Brady installed a Super Bowl countdown clock in his home gym. Each day, he visualized taking his team back to the big game.[7] The next season, the Patriots defeated the Atlanta Falcons 34–28 in Super Bowl LI. Brady has won two more world championships since then—one with the Patriots and another with the Tampa Bay Buccaneers—to bring his record total to seven in his career.

VISION TIP #3:
LET GO OF YESTERDAY

Never let bygones control you. Learn from your mistakes and the hurts others may have caused. Then release them. If you waste too much time gazing in life's rearview mirror, you might become bitter, unmotivated, and depressed. In the process, you'll miss the greater gifts that lie ahead. As the old saying goes, you've got to "keep your eyes on the prize."

Author Stephen King, whose books have sold 350 million copies worldwide, threw his first manuscript into the trash. Fortunately, his wife, Tabitha, retrieved it and urged him to finish the book that would become *Carrie*.[8] Like King, the Detroit rapper Eminem failed miserably at first. He was born to a drug-addicted mother, his father left his family, and he failed the ninth grade three times before dropping out of school. But he never gave up his dream of becoming a rapper, and eventually he won fifteen Grammy Awards and sold more than 220 million records.[9]

A person with vision understands that thinking too much about the drama of the past is like stepping into quicksand. You get pulled in. And if you don't get out in time, you sink. It's best to avoid the trap. Look forward and march on. As author and business leader Stephen Covey says, "Live out of your imagination and not your history."[10]

VISION TIP #4:
BE SERIOUS ABOUT SAVING MONEY

People with a poverty mentality are mired in materialism because they have a fake-it-because-you'll-never-make-it mantra running through their brains. They don't have anything, and they never *expect* to have anything. For them, the only way to feel good is to spend every dime on designer clothes and other adornments that create a facade about their financial well-being. But if you're stashing money away instead of spending it all, you're embracing the possibilities.

Savings are an indication that you're looking toward the future, which is a key component to having a vision and holding it. You're not one of the "sheeple" who graduate from college, get a job, then start the lifelong cycle of earn, spend, earn, spend, earn, spend. You've broken from the visionless cycle of living for the weekend. You understand the adage, "Wealthy people teach their children how to *acquire*. Rich people teach their children how to *sell*. Poor people teach their children how to *buy*." As the billionaire investor Warren Buffett famously said, "Do not save what is left after spending, but spend what is left after saving."[11] Amen.

VISION TIP #5:
BE FLEXIBLE

Tradition is important and new ideas are vital, but the tightrope that binds the two can be a bit wobbly. It's up to you to learn how to balance on it. In other words, you have to decide if you want to blend in and cooperate or go against the status quo and climb out on a limb. I can't tell you the number of times my partners and I had to adjust on the fly when we first started out in business. Think about the number of businesses that had to adjust during the pandemic, whether it was yoga classes and workouts that were being offered online because gyms were closed or restaurants that suddenly had to offer curbside service or delivery. Be prepared to pivot on a moment's notice.

VISION TIP #6:
BE AN OPTIMIST

Have you heard the one about the optimist who goes hunting with a pessimist? The pessimist is trudging along, moping, and the optimist is bounding down a woodsy trail, proudly showing off his beautiful golden retriever. When the two men reach a river, the optimist picks up a stick and throws it as far as he can. The golden retriever jumps in and runs across the top of the water. The pessimist doesn't say a word. So the optimist does it again. He picks up a stick and tosses it into the rippling river. Once again, the dog walks on water and fetches the stick.

The pessimist looks bored, and the optimist can't take it anymore. He looks at the pessimist and asks, "Don't you see anything unusual about my dog?"

The pessimist glares at him. "Sure, I do," he snarls. "He can't swim!"

OK, so it's a corny joke, but it adequately summarizes

the differences in the way people approach life. It's not about what's happening to you; it's the *meaning you give* to what is happening to you. Your perspective can help you rise up, or it can yank you back to the ground. It is all up to you. Are you concentrating on examples of triumph or thinking about a couple of friends who launched small businesses and failed? Are you scouring your circumstances for opportunities and second chances? Or are you pondering everything that could go wrong? Do you see the miracles, or do you see dogs that can't swim?

VISION TIP #7: QUIET TIME

I think this anonymous quote is pretty powerful: "Quiet, calm deliberation disentangles every knot." This means solutions are rarely found in the midst of pandemonium. If you're trying to solve a problem or figure out your next step, it's best to retreat to a silent place. It could be your dorm room (if it's possible to find quiet there) or your apartment (minus the significant other, roommate, and blaring music). Perhaps you could try a chapel, park, or quiet corner of the library. Whatever spot you choose, use that time and space to go inside yourself. That's where the messages are buried, and it's usually the only time those subtle inner voices will come out of hiding. Whether you're praying, meditating, or doing nothing in particular, that peaceful repose will help you clear your mind. You'll get ideas. You'll make decisions. You'll know which deals to consider and which ones to pass up. And for you artistic types, take note: Smokey Robinson, who is considered one of the greatest songwriters of all time, wrote some of his best music while relaxing in his *bathtub*!

VISION TIP #8:
TRAVEL

Get out, see the world, but remember this: when you're traveling, you're taking time out to rest your body—but that doesn't mean you have to shut down your mind. Entrepreneurial vision never takes a holiday. Whether you're touring the ruins of Rome or the pyramids of Egypt, keep scanning your surroundings for hints.

Some friends and I were traveling through Mexico when I saw my first quick-service oil-change shop. I went bonkers over the idea. As soon as I returned to the United States, one of my business partners and I opened one and did exceptionally well financially. I credit my trip for that exposure and stimulation. Nothing revs up your vision like travel. When you're outside your humdrum existence, you're introduced to different ways of thinking and being. The things you see often spark questions that can, in turn, place your life on an entirely new trajectory.

My buddy Ray Snowden is the best proof I have of this belief. He landed a job as a busboy on a cruise ship when he was only seventeen. The ship took him on a magnificent journey on the Great Lakes through Niagara Falls, Buffalo, Chicago, and Milwaukee. Ray was able to meet rich people and observe their way of life. As a result, he became fanatical about etiquette, all the way down to how you eat your soup. Soon he began to adopt that lifestyle and behave as if this had always been part of his world. It gave him confidence that he could hang with established business leaders.

You wouldn't believe the amazing businesses that were hatched while their founders were traveling the world. Logan Green, a college student at the University of California–Santa Barbara, got the idea for a ride-sharing service now called Lyft while traveling with a friend through Namibia, Botswana, and Zimbabwe in Africa in 2005.[12] He noticed that the residents of Zimbabwe didn't drive personal cars and instead used kombis, or shared-rides vans. About a year and a half later, he introduced Zimride to the congested freeways of Los Angeles, and in August 2021, his rideshare company (by then renamed Lyft) was worth an estimated $15.8 billion.[13]

Similarly, the billionaire Richard Branson conceived the concept for Virgin Airlines in the early 1980s because of his flight to his private island in the Caribbean. It seems Branson was on his way to meet a lovely woman when his commercial flight was suddenly canceled. As a solution, Branson, then the thirty-something owner of Virgin Records, leased his own plane. He even borrowed a blackboard and wrote, "Virgin Airlines one-way: $39 to the Virgin Islands."[14] He filled his plane with other passengers whose flights had been canceled. He called Boeing the next day and bought a fleet of 747s. Of course, Branson now has his sights on something even bigger—getting paying customers into space on his Virgin Galactic rocket plane.

VISION TIP #9:
READ

Knowledge is power. Read publications such as the *Wall Street Journal*, the *New York Times*, *Entrepreneur*, *Black Enterprise*, and the *Washington Post*. Subscribe to an online service such as Flipboard, which aggregates stories from around the country and world that are related to topics that interest you. Each morning I read dozens of stories on my Flipboard. Other news aggregator apps include Pocket, Google News, Apple News, and Reddit. They're easy to use, and many of them are free. You'll gain a great deal of information and gather idea after idea. Additionally, I set aside two to three hours each night just for reading. I enjoy some articles and books so much I reread them, discuss them with colleagues, and recommend them to students. One example is the popular *Rich Dad Poor Dad* by Robert Kiyosaki. According to Kiyosaki, the dad with a college degree and a government job that paid quite well didn't achieve nearly as much as the real estate agent dad who was always selling and buying. Although the salesman didn't graduate from college, he became much richer than the one who did. I also recommend *Why "A" Students Work for "C" Students and "B" Students Work for the Government*, also written by Kiyosaki. Both books offer motivational messages that mirror one of my core beliefs: to achieve megasuccess, you don't have to be the sharpest knife in the drawer, but you *do* have to be double-dog daring. You have to have moxie, grit, chutzpah. Remember that having common sense isn't that common nowadays. Book smarts might get you on the dean's list, but street smarts, hard work, and determination are what will make your business successful. There's no use being well educated if you have the survival skills of a poodle.

VISION TIP #10:
HIT THE RESET BUTTON

I have some bad news: a lousy mood can affect your attitude and impact your job performance. The good news is, no matter what's going on, you have the power to change how you're feeling. Instantly. Just repeat an encouraging quote, an inspirational expression, or a snappy line from a song that makes you smile. It could be something fun such as Bruno Mars's "I'm smoother than a fresh jar of Skippy." Or it could be the Reverend Jesse Jackson's emphatic, "I am somebody!" If you're down, put Prince's "Let's Go Crazy" in your ears and tell me you don't feel better instantly. If you find yourself in a state of mind that isn't resourceful, quietly say or sing a positive message to yourself. Whenever I meet a person who is having a rough day, I never allow myself to get drenched in their shower of negativity. I say to myself, "You don't have the power to destroy my joy." That's my reset button.

VISION TIP #11:
WATCH QUALITY TELEVISION

Now, you may be wondering how something as seemingly inane as television made this list. Easy. Because it's not the

TV that's the problem—it's what people are watching. If you turn to public television, you'll learn about history, space, and politics. On CNN, you'll get news from across the world. Meanwhile, C-SPAN reviews books on certain days. On other networks, reporters rove around the planet wandering through remote villages, museums, and castles. Just because you have a TV doesn't mean you have to watch crazy, mindless programs. Black folks watch more TV per hour per capita than any group in America, but a significant number of us are watching trash.[15] What does this have to do with vision? Simple. You will never be what you cannot see.

Instead of wasting your time watching the Kardashians or the housewives of yet another city, watch something meaningful on streaming services or cable TV. Devote your time to watching documentaries about successful entrepreneurs and businesspeople, such as *Inside Bill's Brain: Decoding Bill Gates*, *American Factory*, or *The Pursuit of Happyness*. Go to YouTube and watch a TED Talk. In less than thirty minutes, you can learn about myriad topics such as inspiration, professional growth, collaboration, innovation, communication, and personal growth. The people giving these short presentations are some of the brightest minds in the world. Instead of spending an hour watching some guy trying to survive while naked on a deserted island, spend some quality time learning skills you can actually use.

The bottom line for all eleven of these vision tips is this: *you must see doors where there are no doors.* A leader with vision observes promise in the dust—an abandoned house, a vacant lot, an empty garage in a rundown, inner-city neighborhood. Some of us grew up in tattered houses, while others were raised in sleek homes in the burbs. There's beauty in all of it because, from it, you might be able to sift out memories that could morph into opportunities. You can take the stuff you learned on the streets, clean it up, shine it up, and make it useful to you in a professional context. For example, the Super Soaker, invented by Black nuclear engineer Lonnie Johnson, is no more than an oversized water gun with lots of splash power. I know Johnson personally, and like the rest of us, he used to spend the summers of his childhood chasing his friends with one of those puny, easy-to-break, plastic squirt guns. While the rest of us lamented the limitations of our pretend weapons, he did something about it. Within two years, his ingenious toy had generated $200 million in retail sales.

AVOIDING THE "VISION BUSTERS"

Again, the lesson I want you to take away from this discussion on vision and attitude is that you have to learn how to see opportunities where others can't or won't. If you've grasped that, then you're almost ready for the next step. Before you move on, though, let's go over a few of the pitfalls you'll need to avoid. I call these the "Vision Busters."

Don't Confuse Vision with Living beyond Your Means
Yes, in order to *be it*, you have to *see it*. But don't stretch your imagination so far beyond your budget that you end up in

a financial bind. What you integrate into your life has to be filtered and tempered. If it's not, things can get out of hand. Most risks are planned and calculated. Even a dreamer has to seek balance and know when to act and when to wait.

Don't Leap before You Look

Not every business belongs in every location. Do your homework and assess whether an opportunity is ideal for the venue you have in mind. You wouldn't open a Ben & Jerry's Ice Cream shop in Fairbanks, Alaska, or a rooftop bar with a swimming pool in Seattle. You'd go broke. I know a guy who went to California and saw a Roscoe's chicken restaurant. He came back and announced that he was going to open several Roscoe's in Detroit. I highly advised him against it. Unlike McDonald's or Popeyes's franchises, which are backed by corporations that allow them to become national and international brands, Roscoe's is a local, small-chain business that doesn't transfer well to other cities. Unfortunately, he didn't listen. His three or four Roscoe's restaurants closed within a year. In 2021, Roscoe's House of Chicken 'N Waffles, first founded in 1975, had only seven locations—all of them located in the Los Angeles area. My friend learned the hard way that a great business in one place could be a disaster in another. If he had taken the time to do his due diligence rather than opening four restaurants in a bad market, he'd be in a much different financial position today.

Don't Get in a Familiarity Rut

Step out of your comfort zone. I've met a number of young

business owners who are afraid to stray too far from their roots. They can't think beyond the traditional soul food diner or barbeque shack. This need for familiarity fosters a lack of vision. Some of the most famous brands in the world started as something else. All the ladies out there dreaming of a Tiffany diamond probably didn't know the company actually started as a New York stationery store. Similarly, you may be unaware that Nintendo, the Japanese company behind the Wii, Game Boy, and Switch game systems you probably spend too much time playing, first made old-school playing cards. Those companies obviously took calculated risks and adapted to a changing business world.

I know this lesson well. In 1980, one of the top players at Motorola began experimenting with new communications technology and invited me to join in on their efforts to take cell phones national. But, again, this was 1980. I was still using a phone that had a cord and was hooked to the wall (ask your parents and grandparents). The concept of a phone you could carry in your car or pocket was too foreign to me. I knew about food operation, not burgeoning technology. Because I clung to the familiar, I didn't develop the vision I needed to get in on the ground floor of a sector that was about to explode and would truly change the world.

As Helen Keller, the author and political activist who was deaf, blind, and mute, famously wrote, "The only thing worse than being blind is having sight but not vision." The groundwork for vision is laid when you wake up from society's restrictions on what you can and cannot accomplish.

Sometimes that means doing something no one else has ever attempted. For example, Bob Johnson was working for the Federal Communications Commission (FCC) when he stumbled on information that would revolutionize the world of television. While reading the FCC rules and regulations, he came across a regulation that said underserved communities are eligible for certain opportunities. Johnson went to Viacom with his idea for Black Entertainment Television (BET). He was an upstart who introduced the entertainment industry to a market that had long been neglected. In 2001, Johnson became a billionaire when he sold BET for three billion dollars.

What ideas do you have? What obscure bit of information caught your eye today? What is your vision for the postpandemic world? Are there potential breakthroughs percolating inside you? You are the mover and shaker who can make it all happen by learning to see with something other than your eyes. Take off the blinders. Listen to Usher, who said, "Success is about dedication. You may not be where you want to be or do what you want to do when you're on the journey. But you've got to be willing to have vision and foresight that leads you to an incredible end."[16]

Perhaps Mary McLeod Bethune embodies this best. When Ms. Bethune, an educator, activist, and lecturer, decided she wanted to build a vocational school for girls of color in Winter Haven, Florida, she remembered that Harvey Firestone, Henry Ford, and Thomas Edison wintered there every year. She also knew the Black chauffeur who drove them. After a few efforts, she was able to persuade this driver to bring the three moguls to the parcel of land that would be the site for her new school.

She led them to an empty field, the site of a former city dump.

"I've got my dorms, my girls learning canning and how to be nurses," she said.

Ford, Firestone, and Edison quietly gazed at the barren land. Then Ford leaned over to his two friends and whispered: "You think she's a little feeble?"

They didn't answer for a while, and Ms. Bethune continued her tour.

Finally one of the men called out, "Ms. Bethune, where is this facility?"

She held her head high and responded, "In my mind."

On October 3, 1904, Dr. Bethune started the Daytona Literary and Industrial Training School for Negro Girls. It later merged with the Cookman Institute of Jacksonville, Florida, and became Bethune–Cookman College.

* * *

Surviving the Shift

Who among us wouldn't want to turn back the clock to January 2020 and hit the reset button? Rarely before have we been bombarded with such frightening and depressing news as when coronavirus cases were rising sharply around the world, entire countries were locking down their citizens in quarantine, schools and businesses were closing, and millions of workers were losing their jobs and livelihood as the economy came to a screeching halt. Indeed, it was an extremely scary time for all of us.

As much as anything, we were reminded that we can't do it alone. We had to lean on our support systems to help us make it through each and every day during the pandemic. Just like that complicated toy set we had to assemble in the wee hours of Christmas Eve, mental health isn't a do-it-yourself project. We had to have help to survive the pandemic, whether it was from family, friends, neighbors, our church community, or coworkers—even if we had to receive help from six feet away. After the initial shock of the pandemic, we slowly came to learn that we were all in it together and needed one another to get to the other side.

I leaned on the same people I'd come close to during my professional career, good friends such as Dennis Archer, Ronald Hall, and Roy Roberts. I became exceptionally close to my attorney, Alex Parrish, because I was having to reassess my businesses.

What got me through the dark days of the pandemic wasn't rocket science. It was really just three simple steps:

1. Think positive.
2. Talk positive.
3. Stay positive.

We were all overwhelmed by the pandemic and everything else going on in this crazy world, but staying positive was the only way to get through it. A good attitude means everything.

For many of us, that's easier said than done. An August 2021 poll published by the American Psychological Association found that 32 percent of American adults are so stressed by the pandemic that even daily chores such as choosing what to eat or what to wear are taxing.[17] The poll noted that parents, young adults, and people of color "were more likely to report feeling overwhelmed by such tasks as a result of the pandemic-related stress."[18] It has been very difficult for African Americans and Hispanics, who were hit especially hard by the pandemic.

"We know that they are being disproportionately affected by the pandemic," Vaile Wright, a clinical psychologist and the senior director of health-care innovation at the American Psychological Association, told NBC News. "Dealing with that level of grief, the threat is that much closer for them, and I think that adds an additional level of stress."[19]

The study found that pandemic-related stress led to people avoiding social situations, altering their eating habits, procrastinating, neglecting their responsibilities, and changing their physical activity levels.

Studies have shown that depression and suicide risk among adolescents hit an all-time high during the pandemic. A study conducted by UNICEF on the mental health of adolescents and young people in Latin America and the Caribbean, for example, found that 27 percent reported feeling anxiety and 15 percent struggled with depression.[20] Nearly one-third of the respondents cited their current economic situation as the main reason for anxiety or depression. Nearly half of them reported having less motivation to do activities they typically do, and more than one-third felt less motivated to do daily chores.[21] There's no other way to say it: social isolation, not being in school, not seeing friends, and not participating in sports and other activities had a chilling effect on our young people.

So how do we remain optimistic in such trying times? I came up with eight ways that will hopefully help you maintain your mental health, whether it's a pandemic, difficulties at school or work, or just a daily struggle that might be wearing you down.

1. **Be gracious.** Be thankful for the good things that are happening in your life. My daughter graduated from law school, passed the bar in two states, moved back to Detroit, and now has a job at one of the best firms in the country. It wasn't easy for her, but she put in the hard work and exceeded others' expectations of her. That's something good that happened during the pandemic, and I'm grateful I was around to witness it.

2. **Surround yourself with positive people.** Don't let the Negative Nancies wear you down. If your neighbor only wants to talk about politics and what's wrong in the world, avoid his or her side of the street. And if your Uncle Larry only wants to talk about how much better things used to be, don't sit near him at holiday dinners. Remember that *positive things happen when you distance yourself from negative people.* Don't let others drag you down.

3. **Focus on small things.** As a society, we've become too focused on the endgame or big picture. We need to stop and enjoy what we're doing every day. We need to celebrate the small victories, not just the Super Bowls. Stop worrying about what you might not have and appreciate what you do have.

4. **Look for the silver linings.** It would have been easy for all of us to miss the good things that came out of the pandemic. For a while, though, there was less pollution because fewer people were driving to work, life slowed down a bit, and we learned who and what was important to us. We even became nicer to one another, at least for a while. Remember what the song-writer Leonard Cohen said: "There's a crack in every-thing, that's how the light gets in."[22]

5. **Get off social media.** Much of the stress and anxiety that has engulfed the world is coming from social media such as Facebook and Twitter. It's

not going to do you any good to debate someone you don't know about politics, wearing masks, or getting a vaccine. If you can't get off social media completely, take a break for a few days—or maybe a month. I think you'll be surprised how much better you'll feel.

6. **Take care of yourself.** It wasn't easy to work out and stay in shape during the pandemic. Most gyms were closed and rec leagues canceled seasons. But excercise equipment sales soared, and activities such as outdoor cycling, walking, and golf became more popular than ever. Try yoga and meditation to take the edge off. There's no better way to release stress and anxiety than through a good sweat. Get sleep, eat well, and get some exercise.

7. **Seek help when you need it.** The pandemic has affected people differently. If you're struggling with anxiety or depression, don't be afraid to ask for help. Reach out to a friend, counselor, or pastor. Addressing your mental health is a sign of strength.

8. **Stay in touch with family and friends.** Whether it's by phone, Zoom, or face-to-face meetings, stay connected with family and friends. Schedule a cocktail party on Zoom with your college buddies. We were apart for too long.

Fortunately, I discovered silver linings in my life during the pandemic. I found the cracks that Cohen was talking about. I focused on the positives and maintained an optimistic vision and attitude. While many of my businesses were floundering during the shutdown, my McDonald's franchises were thriving like never before. After a while, people wanted to go out to eat, even if it meant just pulling through a drive-thru. Even in the most difficult times, it's important to have vision and a good attitude. These are essential components of having a million-aire mindset, and you won't thrive and reach your full potential without them.

CHAPTER 3

PRINCIPLE 2:
Prepare for Opportunities

When someone tells me no, it doesn't mean I can't do it.
It simply means I can't do it with them.
—Karen E. Quinones Miller

IN THE EARLY 1900S, hotels didn't allow non-whites. Neither did restaurants and most gas station restrooms. So it wasn't unusual for African American travelers to pack a couple of days' worth of sandwiches and drive all night without stopping. If the journey became too rigorous, they simply pulled alongside the highway and slept in the car, depending on where they were traveling.

Then, in 1936, a New York City postman decided he couldn't take it anymore. Victor H. Green reached out to other mailmen in his network and used their input to compile a list of African American households that were renting out rooms.

Think of it as the Airbnb of the early twentieth century. For people of color, his handy little guide, *The Negro Motorist Green-Book*, became known as the "Green Book," and it was not only valuable—it was a necessity. According to the *Washington Post*, the first guidebook included listings for "hotels, tourist homes, service stations, restaurants, garages, taxicabs, beauty parlors, barbershops, tailors, drugstores, taverns, nightclubs, and funeral homes that welcomed black people at a time in the country when it was legal for establishments to discriminate by race."[1] If you were Black and ready to hit the road, Brother Green's book was your Bible. He may not have fully realized it at the time, but in his state of frustration, he had stumbled on that empty oasis all entrepreneurs seek: the realm of opportunity.

A vital resource was born, all because Green was fed up with sleeping in his car on the side of some dark road. Opportunities are like that. They're not always rare. They're seldom complicated. They're not even that hard to find. Often, they're like the Green Book—the answer to a problem that's right in front of your eyes.

But it's up to you to wake up and take heed. After all, we're living in America, touted as the land of opportunity. This is not the place people flee to so they can scratch their heads and complain that they have no idea how to make money or how to find the doorway to their dreams. If you turn on the six o'clock news, you'll see and hear about a different outlook. While many of us lament that America has seen its best days and grumble about jobs being outsourced to Mexico and Asia, others are devising schemes to get here . . . and get ahead.

Sadly, many of them end up becoming statistics, drowning off the coast of Florida or dehydrating in overheated, poorly ventilated trucks that are sneaking them over the border. But their desperation to reach the Free World suggests there's still something on these shores that makes it worth their while. It's an indication that the economy might have shifted, and banks may not be shelling out big loans, but movers are still moving and shakers are still shaking. It just depends on your focus.

Case in point: When I was in college, one of my room-mates was from Uganda, and he had the oddest comb I'd ever laid my eyes on. It was made of wood and was wide with a stubby handle. Every time he used this comb to groom his hair, I cracked up. Five years later, almost every Black person in America had a plastic version of that Afro pick. Instead of laughing at my African homie, I should have seen the hand-writing on the wall. My former roommate filled a need that I ignored. Later in life, when I traveled to Africa, you better believe I saw business opportunities everywhere, and when I returned to the United States, I was prepared to act on them.

It's sort of like a riddle. All you need to do is survey your surroundings and ask yourself what's missing. While you're complaining about the loss of homegrown opportunities, you might be allowing local and international possibilities to slip through your fingers. Think about it for a moment. In 1945, when John H. Johnson launched *Ebony* magazine, very few publications catered to Black interests. He filled a void. When twenty-one-year-old Ludwick Marishane of South Africa—named Global Student Entrepreneur of the Year in

2011—created a lotion that cleanses the body without water, he filled a void for 2.5 billion people worldwide who lack access to clean water and a sanitary means of bathing. He created the waterless bathing lotion because his best friend was too lazy to bathe. Think about that for a moment: a twenty-one-year-old from Limpopo literally changed the world for billions of people, giving them a better life with his invention.

How about you? What was that last concern you expressed while strolling through your community? Do you see any potential there? What about your friends? Are any of them yearning for a service, an item, a specific brand of clothing? Are your fellow students complaining about anything you can provide?

I once spoke at a historically Black college in Alabama and gave the students the same advice I'm sharing here. One young man reacted in a big way. He noticed that some of the neighboring universities had a population of students who were a bit more affluent that those at the school he attended. Many of those well-heeled students, particularly the freshmen, were fretting over the inconvenience of having to do their own laundry.

The young man sprang into action. He began driving from campus to campus, posting flyers about his laundry pickup business. Later, he drove to the dorms on those campuses, picked up clothes, delivered them to laundry service centers, and returned them—fresh and clean. His company was an instant success! Why? Because one person's curse can be another man's or woman's blessing.

Now, you might be hearing a voice in the back of your head telling you, *I'm only a college student. How am I going to launch a successful business?* It's never too early to start. You might find it hard to believe that college students created many of the most successful websites, including Google, Facebook, Yahoo, and Reddit. Heck, Bill Gates was attending Harvard when he cofounded Microsoft in the late 1970s.[2] Today Gates is the fourth-richest man in the world. Ever read *The Onion* for a good laugh? Two janitors at the University of Wisconsin published the satirical newspaper and distributed it in dorms. Ever call Insomnia Cookies to satisfy your late-night munchies? Seth Berkowitz, who was attending the Wharton School at the University of Pennsylvania, started baking cookies in his dorm room and delivering them to fellow students in 2003.[3] Today, Insomnia Cookies has more than one hundred locations around the country. Each of the aforementioned entrepreneurs recognized a gap in the market and seized the opportunity.

It's all about keeping an open mind. It's all about digging for gold instead of pointing at obstacles. It's all about doing what Booker T. Washington used to preach. During his many lectures, he would encourage his audience to "cast down your bucket where you are." Today that could translate into a pet grooming business, an on-campus manicure service, or a soul food diner near your grandma's church. Or it might mean scrutinizing something outdated and adding a few modern tweaks. I don't know the last time you rode in a cab, but when Uber and Lyft entered the scene, the transportation business changed overnight. These days, when I give talks at colleges, I ask students how many taxicabs Uber owns. The answer, of course, is none.

Uber and Lyft are the perfect examples of companies that revolutionized an industry and practically turned it upside down. It's the largest taxi service in America, yet it doesn't own a single vehicle.

Tell me, how can you be in the transportation business and not own any cars? That's unheard of, isn't it? What's Uber's business model? *Use your own car!* That's why cab companies fought so hard to keep ride-sharing services out of big cities. They knew it would put them out of business. Taxicab owners in New York City were paying anywhere from $450,000 to $700,000 for a taxi medallion. Now Uber comes to town, and anyone with a late model car in good working order can pick up people and knock you out of the game. Even with demand down during the COVID-19 pandemic, Uber's gross revenue reached $21.9 billion in the second quarter of 2021.[4]

Airbnb followed a similar path and process. In 2007, its founders, Brian Chesky and Joe Gebbia, had just moved to San Francisco from New York and were struggling to pay their rent. They recognized that all the city's hotel rooms were being booked during conventions. So they purchased a few air mattresses and advertised an "Air Bed and Breakfast." Their first Airbnb guests were a thirty-year-old Indian man, a thirty-five-year-old woman from Boston, and a forty-five-year-old father of four from Utah.[5] The idea struggled to launch nationwide, but after many starts and stops, Airbnb had more than seven million properties worldwide by 2021. The company says it has generated more than $110 *billion* in earnings for its hosts.

In so many ways, Airbnb is altering the tradition of hotels and motels as we once knew them. Who wants to stay in a small, cramped hotel room when you enjoy the luxuries of someone else's home for the same price? The irony is that when Brother Green was locating accommodations for our mamas, daddies, and grandparents, he was running an Airbnb, old-school style. But he had an unusual goal for an entrepreneur. Green dreamed of a day when his business model would no longer be necessary. By the time he died in 1960, he was pretty close to getting his wish. After the passage of the 1964 Civil Rights Act, Jim Crow laws were gradually abolished and American hotels and restaurants began opening up to people of color. Although the Green Book expanded beyond New York and eventually included most of North America, his family didn't continue it. It is now a faded chapter in Black history, a reminder of the ingenuity of African Americans making a way out of no way.

Yet it's still the original business model for what has become a growing practice of conducting successful enterprises without the brick and mortar. I call the new, nontraditional businesses cyberspace babies. They take emerging technologies and figure out how to marry them with old concepts. For millennial entrepreneurs, the possibilities are infinite. But how do you sift through this sea of trends and come up with something even more innovative? Let's count the ways.

ADOPT OLD IDEAS TO THE LATEST TECHNOLOGY

What did Uber really bring to the party? Cars were already there. People were already there. Uber brought *technology*.

The company created an app. If you're paying attention, you realize that technology is impacting everything, and you're probably wondering where else it can be included and applied. All you have to do is ask the right questions. How is it that the University of Phoenix is one of the largest for-profit universities in the United States, but most of its classes are online? If you see a business lagging behind the times, create something similar but more technologically efficient. Or maybe you can launch a service that shows an existing business how to integrate technology into their services.

Pizza chains such as Domino's, Papa John's, and Little Caesar's, for instance, have been delivering pizzas for decades. But, depending on where you lived, those might have been the only restaurants in town that delivered. Today online delivery platforms such as Uber Eats, Grubhub, and DoorDash can bring just about any type of food to your door—barbeque, burgers, Chinese, Indian, sushi, Mexican, and fast food. They'll even stop at the 7-Eleven for whatever you need. Now *that's* convenience. In the fourth quarter of 2020, when our country was still in the grip of the coronavirus, DoorDash's revenues increased 226 percent to $970 million, and Uber Eats's revenues were up 224 percent to $1.4 billion![6] Most dining rooms were closed, and people were understandably reluctant to eat around others. So, those delivery services brought your favorite foods to you—which in turn generated huge profits for the entrepreneurs who had seen opportunity where others hadn't.

IMPROVE WHAT'S ALREADY THERE

McDonald's owner Ray Kroc was a musician. Let me say that again. The man responsible for the largest restaurant chain in the world had made a living as a performing artist. He supplemented his income by working as a salesman for a company that manufactured the multimixers that are used as shake machines. After a while, he noticed something interesting. He sold more cups for these machines to a small restaurant in a California town called San Bernardino than anywhere else in the country. Curiosity got the best of him, and Kroc made it his business to find out why. He flew to California to meet with the McDonald brothers and discovered that they were doing a brisk business selling nothing but burgers, fries, soft drinks, and shakes. The line wrapped around the counter. Intrigued, Kroc asked the brothers if they wanted to expand and take their vision around the country. They weren't interested but allowed Kroc to develop the plan and pay them 1 percent of the sales. Eventually, Kroc bought them out completely, and the popular eatery exploded into the international chain that millions of people frequent today.

Another excellent example of a business that improved an existing industry is Netflix. For years, Americans flocked to box stores such as Blockbuster to rent VHS tapes and then DVDs of movies to watch on the weekends. This was before movies were initially launched on HBO and Cinemax or on other streaming services. Netflix changed the game in 1997 when it allowed customers to rent or purchase DVD movies.

Then it offered subscriptions that allowed customers to rent as many DVDs as they wanted, before eventually transitioning entirely to a streaming service. Today Netflix is worth an estimated $200 billion,[7] and at last count there was exactly one Blockbuster store still open in Bend, Oregon.

PRACTICE "TWO-ARMED" LIVING

I can't take credit for this one. It belongs to my witty, high-spirited granddaddy. Whenever someone had a job and recognized opportunities to do business with those he worked with, my granddaddy used the "two-armed living" expression. Others call it a "side hustle." It's actually a pretty innovative approach to business. For instance, I know of a schoolteacher who taught shop, carpentry, and auto mechanics. Half of the employees at the school were women, and many of them were single. In their apartments, they needed shelves installed, pictures mounted, and more. So the shop teacher used his own resources to create a carpentry business on the side. While the other teachers drove standard cars, he made so much money he bought a canary yellow Corvette.

MAKE ALL SITUATIONS SERVE YOU

What did we do before Post-it Notes? We jotted things down haphazardly here or there. It was a hodgepodge system that led to a lot of lost messages and one big mess. Enter Arthur Fry, an engineer for 3M, formerly known as the Minnesota

Mining and Manufacturing Company. He was also active in his church and fond of his role of singing in the choir. In that role, he was constantly frustrated by page markers that kept slipping out of place, making it hard for him to find the right songs in his hymnal. It seemed silly at first, but he decided to try some of the adhesive created by his colleague, Spencer Silver. Voilà! Although the adhesive had been deemed a failure at 3M because it wasn't strong enough for industrial uses, it was the perfect solution to Fry's problem. He returned to the office and explained that, when used properly, the glue was quite functional. By making the best of an awkward situation, Fry came up with a clever little item that many companies now consider an essential tool. Post-it Notes are one of the top-five bestselling office supply products in the world.

BE OBSERVANT

Some think of people-watching as a mindless activity. But I know of someone who did it so much he discovered an opportunity. He was an employee at a small regional airport when he noticed that nothing upset travelers more than losing their luggage. After he retired, he contacted a friend who served on the aviation committee for the board of the city's airport authority. His friend gave him the inside scoop on how to bid on contracts to deliver lost bags. The retired guy bid and got nowhere. He tried again the next year, and then again the year after. Finally, after years of persistence, he landed a contract that allowed him to pick up misplaced bags and deliver them to distraught travelers. It turned into a profitable business with low overhead. All he needed was an SUV, a tank of gas, and four or five buddies who wanted to make extra money on the side.

FIND AN UNMET NEED AND FILL IT

I live in a community that has a special arrangement with the police department. If a resident goes out of town, he or she can leave keys and information about their whereabouts so the police can provide special security at their home. One day, one of the officers knocked on my door and said he was planning to retire and launch a business that was more extensive than the standard police department patrols. For a fee, the retired officer would make daily surveillances inside the homes of people who would be out of town for an extended period. Well, several years ago while I was out of town, the pipes burst in my home's steam sauna. However, very little damage occurred because the officer caught the problem on the second day of a long trip. Sometimes I'm gone for an extended period of time. My house could have been a total wreck. This business filled an important need. Given my frequent travel schedule, his offer met a huge need I didn't even know I had.

You might be surprised that many of the most profitable small businesses in 2021 met specific needs in their communities. If you didn't notice, the price of a new car, truck, or SUV skyrocketed during the COVID-19 pandemic. People are holding on to their current vehicles longer, which created greater demand for auto repair shops. Like food delivery services, food trucks have also become increasingly popular. You can order at the truck and eat outdoors, avoiding indoor dining rooms. Mobile car wash services that come to you have also been successful, along with personal training, personal wellness, and babysitting. With so many people working from home nowadays, they're looking for people to watch their kids and tutor and teach them at home. Demand for mobile apps and technology geared toward kids is also sharply on the rise.

Vegetarian restaurants have been around for a while, but who would have thought we'd see restaurants that catered specifically to vegans—people who eat no meat or animal by-products, including dairy and eggs? And who would have thought that you could walk into a major chain restaurant and ask for gluten-free food? There are even restaurants that are *entirely* gluten-free. If you're interested in opening a food establishment, study the trends and determine where there's a demand or untapped niche. If you live in a neighborhood or town with four Mexican restaurants, chances are it doesn't need another one. The same goes for barbeque and pizza.

FOLLOW YOUR PASSION

I'm sure you've tried Mrs. Fields cookies at least once in your life. But did you know she started out as a California house-wife who enjoyed whipping up batches of cookies and selling them around her subdivision in Palo Alto? She even went to banks with fresh cookie samples and a business plan, trying to secure a loan to open a cookie business. However, after eating all her cookies, the bankers refused her loan request. After being continually denied a bank loan that would have helped her purchase ovens, Mrs. Fields thought about the fact that most churches had kitchens but used their ovens only once or twice a week. She contracted with thirty churches before finally securing a loan with 21 percent interest. Today, Mrs. Fields Famous Brands, parent to the TCBY yogurt and Mrs. Fields cookie chains, has more than five hundred retail outlets, over three hundred franchises, and a net worth of more than $45 million.

CREATE YOUR OWN OPPORTUNTIES

No matter what route you take, remember one thing: ingenuity is the midwife of opportunity. This is one of my most fervent beliefs. I don't believe in the word *no*, and I have the utmost respect for go-getters like Ray Kroc, Victor Green, and Mrs. Fields. As James Brown used to sing, "I don't want nobody to give me nothing. Open up the door and I'll get it myself."[8]

It just so happens that some people were at the right door at the right time. I was one of those people. My friends and I were probably the ninth Black group in the country to open a new McDonald's franchise. That was a huge feat, and it's a milestone I might not have been able to reach in a different country and at a different point in history.

It's well-known in certain parts of the world, if your daddy is a butcher, you would more than likely become a butcher. Not so in the United States. My father was a good man, but he never achieved a fraction of the success I have obtained. I believe that may be due, in part, to a special "door" that opened and allowed me to "get in myself." I'm not diminishing my credentials. But I honestly don't feel a Bill Pickard–type would have become the owner of a McDonald's franchise without a fleeting moment in time labeled *affirmative action*. Affirmative action is a set of government and private sector policies and practices created in response to a lopsided and unfair playing field in a country that had denied opportunities to Blacks for centuries. It was a way to eliminate the "good ol' boy network" that was prevalent in the business world. When I came along, there was a great deal of pressure from Black political leaders such as Detroit mayor Coleman Young to open up opportunities for Black suppliers, dealers, foremen, and apprentices.

Note that I have never viewed affirmative action as a plan based on quotas; it was no more a quota system than Harvard or Yale's archaic admissions policies of the past. If they had admitted students based on test scores, Asians would have made up 40 to 60 percent of the student body. That's what I say to people who try to suggest that affirmative action and quotas are synonymous. If those same individuals are so opposed to quotas, then why do they support legacy admissions at a large number of institutions, including some of the top universities in the country?

The bottom line is that certain individuals were given a boost, and I was one of them. In America, the doors of opportunity swung open around 1968. If you could walk, talk, and chew bubble gum as a proactive Black person, you had a good chance of boarding the train that led to the right jobs, loans, grants, and business contracts. If you had that same level of ambition in the 1950s, it didn't matter. African Americans were still being relegated to the lowest rung of the social ladder. Back then, some Black women with bachelor's degrees landed jobs as teachers. But many were working as domestics while Black men with similar credentials were working in the post office.

Fortunately, that era was replaced by two decades of affirmative action, business set-asides (when the government reserves contracts for goods and services to minority-owned businesses), and other incentives. Unfortunately, those days are gone. When the 2008 financial crisis and recession swept the country, cutbacks ensued and the landscape of abundance began to shrink. The coronavirus pandemic only exacerbated the climate. In 1966, if you knocked on the door of an extremely affluent family in Michigan, you wouldn't have had any problem enlisting their support for an important cause. The white man who opened the door probably worked at General Motors, and his children might have attended the University of Michigan and had good summer jobs. Today, try knocking on the same door and he will respond, "Do you realize my son-in-law has an MBA from Northwestern University and can't get a job in his field?" Hence, he'd be less likely to consider sponsoring a scholarship program for minorities or other projects designed to address economic and social disparities. This is what has happened to America. It's divided. It's lethargic and apathetic. It's been lulled into an everyone-for-themselves mentality. That's never been truer than it is today.

But these barriers are not impenetrable. Those bent on success simply have to be more self-reliant and creative. I saw a wonderful illustration of this while attending an automobile show in Germany and noticed an SUV with a mirror attached to the driver's side—inside. This was in addition to the standard-issue vanity mirror on the passenger side. I was taken aback. When I inquired about the purpose of the extra interior mirror, a representative explained that it allowed the drivers to check on children sitting in the back seat. I smiled and asked, "What lady invented that?" The guy laughed. He and I both realized that, although the device was functional, most men never would have thought of it.

That was opportunity. That was a woman's intuition. That was a woman being a mother. I often refer to this story when I talk about diversity because it demonstrates how a company—and its bottom line—can benefit from what everyone is bringing to the table. I'm not a gambling man, but I'm willing to bet several male engineers could have worked on the same SUV but would not have walked out of that design session with the brilliant and groundbreaking idea of a mirror that allowed drivers to keep an eye on their children.

This is evidence of the growing demand for gender-blind opportunities. In the 1950s, if you went to New York University, Columbia University, or the University of Michigan, you might have found that, among the students enrolled in the masters of business administration, medical, or dental programs, fewer than 10 percent were women. If you visited those same schools in 2021, you would find a much higher representation of female students. At NYU, for example, 41 percent of the first-year students in the MBA program were women in the class of 2023.[9] What changed? Have women become smarter or have men become more enlightened? The opportunities are there, and they were not there before. It's as simple as that. Once the opportunities surfaced, so did the female students. They were already prepared, just like they were in 1950. Yet the system comprising primarily white men wouldn't give them a chance.

What do you do in a situation like that? What if—due to age, gender, or race—you are being blocked from the circumstances that yield success? Well, this is where I resort to platitudes. Work five times harder. Be better than the best. Believe in yourself. Carve out opportunities where there are no opportunities. And, last but not least, when your big break finally presents itself, make sure you don't make the common mistakes that can chase it away. In other words, don't ruin your chances by committing the following "opportunity errors."

OPPORTUNITY ERROR 1:
BRAGGING

If you have the bragging habit and refuse to kick it, you're setting yourself up for rejection after rejection. You'll lose clients and destroy meaningful relationships that could have helped you farther down the road. Believe in yourself, but at the same time, be modest. It's common sense. Remember, no matter how big your house is, how nice your car is, or how big your bank account is, our graves will always be the same size. Stay humble.

OPPORTUNITY ERROR 2:
GIVING UP TOO SOON

During the California Gold Rush, droves of people went west in search of their fortune. Some of them claimed a plot of land and worked it feverishly for five or six years, but to no avail. Feeling defeated, they sold their plots for about $100, returned home, and found a job in a meatpacking plant. Six months later, a few of them received a letter that caused their jaws to drop and their hearts to sink. The person who bought their plot had just struck gold. This is a true scenario and a powerful testament to the importance of never giving up. What if Michael Jordan had quit after being cut from his high school varsity team? It was the GOAT himself who famously said, "Obstacles don't have to stop you. If you run into a wall, don't turn around and give up. Figure out how to climb it, go through it, or work around it."[10]

OPPORTUNITY ERROR 3:
HITCHING YOUR WAGON
TO THE WRONG DREAM

Don't open a burger joint at a commune for vegans. OK, this is a far-fetched example, but you get my point. Test the market. Do your due diligence. Also, be authentic to yourself and make sure the opportunity is the right fit. I was once offered a job as associate director of the US Small Business Administration in Washington, DC. I turned it down. The job paid around $100,000 a year, but at the same time I was on the fast track with my McDonald's franchises. Meanwhile, another individual who was more politically connected than I was at the time accepted a similar position. Four years later, he resigned and built an impressive company based on contracts from the Department of Defense, the Federal Aviation Administration, and others. He later sold his company for more than $200 million. It's important to note that he was a political operative and a Washington insider. I was neither. At the time, each of us decided to stay in our lanes and did what we were most comfortable doing. I could have made the decision he did and failed miserably, and he could have opened a McDonald's franchise and not been successful. Instead, each of us became a winner in our respective fields.

OPPORTUNITY ERROR 4:
FALSE PRIDE

If you want to get ahead in the modern workplace, be willing to start at the bottom. That's one of my biggest complaints of young people today. So many think they're entitled to start at the top or near the top without putting in the blood, sweat, and tears to get there. Sure, you have big plans. But along the way, you might have to mop a few floors or flip a few burgers. I did both. In the end, it all paid off. Yet I know of more than one instance in which people turned down business offers because they didn't want to start on the low rung of the ladder. They kept their sights on executive positions within leading corporations. Sadly, their attempts to start at the top didn't go too well, and their dreams never materialized. The lesson here is simple—a little humility never hurt anyone.

In Detroit, there was a fifty-six-year-old man who walked eight hours covering twenty-one miles to and from work every day because he couldn't afford a car. He did this even in blizzard conditions and subzero-degree weather. Somehow, the local newspaper discovered his situation and sent a reporter out to interview him. The story went viral. Eventually, three GoFundMe pages were established to help him. They raised more than $35,000, and he ended up with a nice, suburban apartment that was closer to his job and a brand-new Ford Taurus. There are myriad other examples of good people leaving a struggling waitress a $1,000 tip, teachers rallying to help a custodian, or strangers helping out a college student who is struggling to pay tuition and other living expenses. The bottom line: people like to help others who are working hard and striving to make their dreams come true. Americans still appreciate honest, hard work.

I see it like this: there are always opportunities being born and opportunities yet to be made—but you have to push your-self and get involved in making them happen. Lolly Daskal, president and CEO of Lead from Within, explains it this way: "Opportunities are in front of you everyday, but to see them you need to look at the world as a place of hope and possibility, not limits, obstacles, and problems."[11]

It's so easy to say to yourself, *I don't have any money. I don't have any resources. I don't have any of these things I see in the* Wall Street Journal, Town & Country, Vanity Fair, Black Enterprise, Essence, *or on TV. How am I ever going to build a business?* But while you're drowning yourself in self-doubt and busily listing all the reasons why you can't do it, there is someone else who's worse off than you and yet who is doing it, even as you read these words. And there's someone who did it long ago when her only hope was prayer and a bended knee.

In the post–Civil War era, that someone was the daughter of former slaves. At a time when her peers were doing anything they could to survive, she proudly made the declaration, "I don't want to work for no White folks, and I don't want to work in nobody's kitchen." In 1901, Lillian Harris Dean, later referred to as Pig Foot Mary, migrated from Mississippi to New York with nothing but pennies in her pocket and a whole lot of determination in her soul.

Grudgingly, she accepted a job as a domestic, but as soon as she earned a grand total of $5, she bought a baby buggy and loaded it up with her good-tasting, down-home foods. She would stand on a Harlem street corner from sunup to sundown, selling pig's feet and hog maws out of that beat-up baby carriage. There were other folks, just like her, who'd fled to the North in search of a better life. The way Pig Foot Mary saw it, they missed their mama's cooking, and it would be real easy to tempt them with the sassy aroma of her hot, smoking chitlins and sizzling corn on the cob.

Her plan worked like a charm. In no time at all, she was able to purchase a steamer and park it near a newsstand across from a local saloon. Plenty of Blacks hung out there and became her loyal patrons. By 1929, Mary had amassed $375,000—no small task for an illiterate, uneducated Black woman who was raised in a shack. In today's market, that $375,000 would be equivalent to $5.7 million.

Remember that the next time you ask, "Where are the opportunities?" Think about the resolve of Pig Foot Mary and then tell yourself, "Proactivity is opportunity's accountability partner."

* * *

Surviving the Shift

There's no question that the worldwide COVID-19 pandemic has greatly altered the way we live and work.

Now, instead of jumping on a train or in an Uber to go to the office each day, we're working from our kitchen tables, home offices, or wherever we can get a suitable Internet connection. Instead of dining out with family and friends, we're eating in with food that is delivered to our front doors or picked up from the local grocery stores or restaurants via curbside service. We used to go to the movies to see the latest hits from Hollywood, but now we're bingeing new releases and TV shows through streaming channels such as Netflix and Hulu.

Our world has changed dramatically, and it might never go back to the way it was before.

How businesses operate and how consumers act have changed significantly as well. A May 2021 study by the McKinsey Global Institute found that e-commerce surged like never before during the pandemic, increasing its share of total retail sales in the United States by more than three times.[12] In fact, the report noted that "first-time online grocery shoppers accounted for 30 to 50 percent of total U.S. consumers shopping online in July 2020, driven largely by baby boomers nudged by the pandemic to make a digital transition they otherwise might not have needed to make."[13] Home nesting, telemedicine, virtual health care, and remote education also took off as people were stuck at home.

So the big question for you, my friends, is what new opportunities are out there for the want-to-be entrepreneurs? What necessity can you bring to your community, like Victor H. Green did for African American travelers all the way back in 1936? How can you fill a specific need the way Uber, Lyft, Insomnia Cookies, and Airbnb did so successfully?

While the pandemic had a devastating effect on Black-owned businesses, it also created new pathways to owning a business. According to research by Robert Fairlie, an economics professor at the University of California Santa Cruz, about 40 percent of Black-owned businesses closed in the immediate aftermath of the pandemic, which was about twice as high as all active US companies.[14]

Yet the silver lining is that many people who lost their jobs and were out of work decided to become entrepreneurs. The *New York Times* reported in May 2021 that new business registrations more than doubled in the months after the CARES Act was signed in March 2020 and then rose again in December 2020 and March 2021, when the federal government issued more stimulus payments.[15] A Kauffman Foundation study found that about 380 out of every 100,000 Black adults became entrepreneurs during the pandemic.[16]

"The idea that the pandemic has kind of restarted America's start-up engine is a real thing," Scott Stern, an economist at MIT, told the *New York Times*. "Sometimes you need to turn off the car in order to turn it back on."[17]

So after having our world turned upside down by

the coronavirus, let's reexamine the ways millennial entrepreneurs can come up with innovative ideas to start new businesses.

ADOPT OLD IDEAS TO THE LATEST TECHNOLOGY

How many people do you know who plunked down a few thousand dollars to buy a Peloton bike or treadmill during the pandemic? With gyms and YMCAs closed during the pandemic, consumers sought safe alternatives for working out at home. In September 2020, Peloton announced its first-ever quarterly profit, which came after a 172 percent increase in sales.[18] The home-fitness company reported that more than one million people were subscribing to its online fitness classes, and the average number of monthly workouts had doubled to about twenty-five classes per subscriber. Not surprisingly, Peloton's stock shares increased by 220 percent in 2020.[19]

Obviously, most start-ups aren't going to be the scale of worldwide companies like Peloton. Here's a great example of a smaller start-up that adopted old ideas to new technology. Marie E. Saint-Cyr was born in Haiti and immigrated to the United States when she was eight years old. She participated in art programs as a child and studied at the Fashion Institute of Technology and at the Lorenzo de' Medici Institute in Florence, Italy.

Initially, Saint-Cyr wanted to make sure young people

had access to art programs the way she did. She pitched the idea of having an art camp during winter break for children. An organization told her to come up with a budget, and it would pay her to organize and manage the camp. When the pandemic hit, the children could no longer attend the camp in person. So she recorded thirty-minute art lessons. When she had about seventy-five lessons in her catalog, she came up with the idea of licensing them to hospitals and long-term care homes. She even sold individual art kits for patients and residents at the facilities.

"Because I was an artist, I always had the mindset that if the opportunity isn't there, just create it, which is something I've always done," she said. "I feel like as a result of all the programs I've been doing, I'm constantly seeing opportunities where someone may be already doing something, but I can add to it, or someone isn't doing something there at all."[20]

In 2021, the Saint-Cyr Art Studio also became a mural company that designs and manages mural projects for corporations, schools, health-care facilities, state agencies, nonprofits, and other groups. Some of her clients include MasterCard, New York City Department of Transportation, and CJ Foods.

"Being someone who grew up in Haiti, that kind of teaches you resourcefulness, so I have the mindset that if something isn't there, just be resourceful," Saint-Cyr said. "If the opportunity isn't there, create it for yourself. If you see something that can be improved, go for it."[21]

IMPROVE WHAT'S ALREADY THERE

Every day, more than sixty million plastic bottles end up in landfills and incinerators—a total of about twenty-two billion per year, according to the Container Recycling Institute.[22] In some cities in America, there isn't a safe alternative to bottled water. Just ask the residents of Flint, Michigan, and Benton Harbor, Michigan.

David M. Walker, an attorney in Atlanta, is trying to solve this crisis. He launched StarWalker Industries with the goal of reducing the amount of plastic being dumped in landfills and on the streets by building sustainable, closed-loop bottled water recycling plants. Essentially, his company is paying people to bring back their used bottles to be recycled into new bottles.

If that sounds ambitious, Walker has another vision for his life: he wants to win a Super Bowl as an NFL team owner. Like Madam C. J. Walker's vision board we discussed in the previous chapter, the Super Bowl trophy keeps David Walker focused on what he wants to achieve.

"I just go trophy case shopping every now and then," David Walker said. "I do agree that you've got to have something every day to sort of remind you of the grind you're in from a 10,000-foot view."[23]

BE OBSERVANT

When Americans couldn't leave their homes during the pandemic, they turned to a furry and lovable source of comfort—cats and dogs. A survey by the American Pet Products Association found that pet ownership in the United States rose to an all-time high of 70 percent in 2020.[24] Guess what? People who were working from home for a year and a half now need dog walkers, groomers, and boarding services as they slowly return to the office.

Bloomberg Businessweek reported that Americans acquired forty-seven million pets in 2020, and as those dogs and cats mature, the pet-care business is expected to almost triple to $275 billion by 2030.[25] Be observant of trends like this and figure out how to profit from it. I know some people who probably prefer their pets over their significant others (or even their children), and they'll spend whatever it takes to pamper their cats and dogs.

FIND AN UNMET NEED AND FILL IT

Even when COVID-19 is a distant memory, there are going to be certain people who are reluctant to go out into the world the way they did before. Whether it is because of underlying health conditions or their age, some people simply aren't going to frequent bars, restaurants, movie theatres, and other places like they used to. That's going to create a need for delivery services in certain communities, whether it's delivering food, snacks, groceries, medicine, or whatever. Not every town or neighborhood is big enough to sustain a delivery service such as Uber Eats or DoorDash. Do some digging and determine if your hood needs a delivery service.

MAKE ALL SITUATIONS SERVE YOU

As a kid growing up in Atlanta, Corey Ackerman noticed something strange in the stores where he and his family shopped: there weren't a lot of goods specifically tailored to African American consumers. So Ackerman decided to do something about it, even while he was still attending college. He opened a home decor and gift business, selling everything from wall art, mirrors, clocks, figurines, stationery, and gifts. Today, LeRoi Products does business with national chains such as Family Dollar, Walmart, HomeGoods, T. J. Maxx, and online sites such as Wayfair.com.

"The greater vision has not changed," Ackerman said. "The idea that there could be an African American boy or girl who sees a positive image of themselves in products on the shelves, whether that be a birthday balloon, greeting card, or a piece of artwork, that still touches home for me."[26]

During the pandemic, large retail chains that hadn't purchased goods from LeRoi Products in the past were suddenly reaching out to him. Part of it was a greater awareness of Black consumers, for sure, but the nationwide supply chain problems also sent retailers scurrying to suppliers who had goods on hand, including Ackerman.

"There is a shortage of a lot of things," Ackerman said. "And so where there wouldn't ordinarily be people like divisional merchandise managers or buyers for major distribution reaching out to you—you'd be reaching out to them—now they're reaching out to you because they're kind of in a panic mode. We've seen what's happened with the automotive industry. We've seen what's happened with appliances and a number of other industries, not just those. And so I think that the opportunity is that if there is a big client, if there is someone that you want to get in the door of, now is the time to get in that door because they need product and they need it from people who can get it to many, many doors very quickly."[27]

When other companies weren't able to fill needs, Ackerman stepped up and got his merchandise into new outlets. As Warren Buffet famously said, "It's good to learn from your mistakes. It's better to learn from other people's mistakes."[28]

There were a couple of stories I read during the pandemic that reaffirmed my belief in the resolve of the American worker. Pilar Donnelly of Houston had been laid off from her job in sports marketing. As her twin boys were about to celebrate their sixth birthday, she wanted to build them something that would keep them entertained while they were at home during the pandemic. Her idea ended up becoming a successful business.

Even though Donnelly had never used a power tool and didn't have any experience in woodworking, she decided she would build her boys a custom playhouse. She watched a few YouTube videos to learn techniques and then set out to complete the project. Donnelly shared her progress through photos on social media, and before long she had others asking her to build them playhouses, she sheds, bunk beds, and other projects. Wish You Wood Custom Creations was born![29]

Like Donnelly, LaShone and RaeShawn Middleton, thirty-year-old identical twins from Washington, DC, lost their jobs as a result of the pandemic. In fact, they were laid off from their jobs as servers at different restaurants within a few hours of each other. When they had a craving for blue crabs on a rainy night, they did not want to go out and there was no blue crab delivery service in their area. They saw a need and created the idea of delivering crabs cooked or frozen from online orders. The twins now have locations in Maryland and Washington, DC, (carryout and delivery only). The crabs are available frozen or cooked, and they want to expand further. One day, they want to have their own kitchen and multiple locations, according to the *Los Angeles Times*.[30]

That's what I call hustling!

CHAPTER 4

PRINCIPLE 3:
Look for Finance Options Everywhere

*A big part of financial freedom is having your heart
and mind free from worry about the what-ifs of life.*
—Suze Orman

HER WORDS RANG in my ear, and I listened patiently. I didn't agree with what she was saying, but this was my mama speaking, and even in my advanced years, I wasn't about to talk back. "Boy, you're crazy," she said in the sharpest tone. "You're working too hard. Money can't make you happy."

I gazed at my dear old mother fondly and nodded my head. I never told her what I was thinking that day, but if I had it would have sounded something like this: "No ma'am, money can't buy happiness, but it's certainly a good down payment."

After I had attained a certain level of wealth, many of my

conversations with my mother began and ended that way. She would warn me about the evils of money, and I would respond with silent respect. I understood the source of her suspicions, and I didn't want to make her think I had strayed from my home training.

For the record, I'm not obsessed with money. It's not that big of a deal to me. However, I do put it up there with oxygen and water. I agree with Kendrick Lamar: "Money trees [are] the perfect place for shade."[1] Just make sure you water and nurture your money tree, so it grows bigger and bigger. I'm also the first to point out that money is not the root of all evil, as some people believe. On the contrary, the *lack* of money is the root of all evil. Not having money can lead to despair, desperation, depression, sickness, and abject poverty. As Big WoRm said, "Playing with my money is like playing with my emotions."[2] But while the lack of money is a dream killer, money in abundance can be misunderstood, abused, and even feared. Secretly, people see it as the stuff of sorcerers, the nectar of kings and queens. It's shrouded in mystery and wrapped up in ancient folklore. Genies arise from lanterns and reward people with it. Pirates spent their entire lives searching for treasure chests. The children of the rich and famous have it bestowed on them at birth.

So it's no surprise when a would-be entrepreneur gets caught up in the hype. I'm referring to those inexperienced up-and-comers who tend to hesitate or make excuses. If this describes you, then here's a quick question: when the business climate seems inviting and opportunities are rising like a tide over a moonlit sea, why do you freeze and grab a life preserver? Why aren't you jumping in headfirst? The answer: You're eager to launch a business, but you can't seem to stop fretting about one key component—seed capital. You're wondering where it is and how you're going to get it. The magical allure of money has you under its spell, and you have convinced yourself that you'll never be able to acquire the revenue needed to get your operation off the ground.

You are not alone. The thought of seeking a loan is intimidating enough to make the average aspirant drop the notion altogether. More often than not, people with great ideas never pursue them because they think of money as an insurmountable hurdle. A survey conducted by Qualtrics found that 32 percent of Americans considered starting a business, but the majority of them never did anything to get their start-up off the ground. The reason probably isn't a surprise—42 percent said they didn't have the money to get started.[3]

I'm here to tell you, my friend, that nothing could be further from the truth.

Notice I said the "thought" of securing funds is intimidating. The reality is another story. Financing is actually the easiest aspect of entrepreneurship. Yes, you're reading that correctly. I'm telling you to relax. Funding is as simple as the alphabet and far more accessible than you think.

I know that sounds like an outrageous claim. However, everything is financeable. Most good ideas get financed. And a lot of bad ideas get financed. There's a guy in Michigan who has a reputation for investing in almost anything. Years ago, someone came up with the unusual notion that gas station pumps should include speakers and video screens that broadcast advertisements. Most investors found the concept, well, different. But if you think about it, the idea was brilliant. People have to refuel their cars and trucks four or five times every month or they can't go anywhere. Nearly 90 percent of service stations are open twenty-four hours a day, and it takes about seven to nine minutes to fill a tank. The target audience can't go anywhere. The next thing I knew, commercials were airing every time I lifted the lever of a gas pump at a suburban station. You guessed it—the investor (who shall remain unnamed) financed the deal. So you see, all you have to do is be inventive, flexible, and fearless.

Nearly all entrepreneurs start out with no money. Many of them are just as broke as the next person. Yet they achieve their goals anyway. As my grandmother used to explain, "You take one step, and God will take two." That's another way of saying, "Go forth with your business plans and, sooner or later, the money will appear." With that said, I must warn you that most start-ups are not financed by banks. Instead, start-ups are funded by a host of alternative sources. My situation is an ideal example. The McDonald's opportunity surfaced while I was still working on a PhD at Ohio State University. My Alpha Phi Alpha fraternity brothers urged me to take out a loan, and I heeded their advice. I have already shared this story, but it bears repeating because it demonstrates how smooth the process can be. You see, that $10,000 loan changed my life and forever altered the way I view finance options.

It was a hefty chunk of cash that helped me get my foot in the door of the world of free enterprise. But here's the memory that makes me want to shout from the mountaintops—I didn't have to pay back all the debt. The loan conditions stated that 10 percent would be forgiven every year I worked in a public education institution. So, of course, I took a job teaching at Wayne State University in Detroit, and when I walked out several years later, almost half of my loan was paid off.

So allow me to reiterate: finance is the easiest part of the entrepreneurial adventure.

FUNDING YOUR ENDEAVOR

Most of us don't come from families that can write us a one-million-dollar check and tell us to get out in the world and make our mark. That's only for the truly privileged and Hollywood. But we have at our fingertips a supreme resource called *creativity*. Numerous studies have shown that children who grow up in families where there was an entrepreneur are more inclined to become entrepreneurs. If you have this advantage, then build on it. If not, follow the examples set by parents, grandparents, aunts, and uncles who had to borrow from Peter to pay Jamal and juggle what little they had left.

THE THREE Fs

How is it that Big Mama always came up with the money to get June Bug out of jail? Figure out how she maneuvered, then do it yourself. In most cases, that means turning to the same sources our ancestors relied on—the Three Fs:

1. Friends

2. Family

3. Fools

Do not underestimate these Three Fs. When you're starting out, the people in your immediate circle will be your cheering squad and number one financers. Surprisingly, many of them will be far more willing to chip in than you ever imagined.

Budding entrepreneurs turn to friends and family because they're the people who tend to believe in them when no one else does, and they'll offer whatever assistance they can. In 1959, Berry Gordy Jr. took out an $800 loan from his family—his father owned convenience stores and insurance and construction companies—and founded Motown Records in 1959.[4] That's right, the man who gave us The Supremes, The Four Tops, The Jackson 5, Stevie Wonder, Marvin Gaye, and so many others relied on the first of Three Fs to finance the start of Hitsville, USA. Do you know what other companies were started with loans from family members? Amazon, Chipotle, GoPro, Tesla, Applebee's, Friendly's Ice Cream, and Jimmy John's, to name a few.

And do I have to explain fools? They're those starry-eyed individuals who will dig into their pockets whenever they hear about anything that sounds remotely promising. Either that or they like to gamble every chance they get. Go ahead, give them their chance.

But there is one "chance" I urge you to avoid at all costs: payday loans. These unregulated loans typically offer a minimal amount of money with outrageously high interest rates, and they must be paid off by the time you receive your next paycheck. Stay away from payday loans and other bottom feeders that will leave you mired in exorbitant fees and other pitiful circumstances. There are better alternatives out there, no matter what your situation is. Although many states have implemented regulations to protect consumers from predatory lenders, it's still legal in states such as Alabama to charge as much as 17.5 percent on a $500 loan, which must be repaid in ten to thirty-one days. Let me do the math for you: you're going to pay $87.50 for a $500 loan.

And while you're at it, don't depend solely on grants. I frequently get asked about grants for entrepreneurs. I used to reply, "As soon as I ever find out about a grant, after I get mine, I'm going to call you." Today, a seismic shift has occurred. Some *legitimate* grants and government-assistance programs have sprung up, especially during the COVID-19 pandemic. However, your own savings, if you have them, is the primary revenue stream with absolutely no strings attached. Many entrepreneurs draw their initial seed capital from personal bank accounts they have strategically grown over the years. Other entrepreneurs do a considerable amount of research and dig up a host of unconventional lending options.

COMMUNITY DEVELOPMENT CORPORATIONS

Just as the name suggests, community development corporations are responsible for community services as well as affordable housing. They will also fund businesses that fit their mission, as long as the business is located within certain zip codes. If the company you're starting is considered an enhancement or service to a designated urban or rural area, a community development corporation may be a solution for you.

Remember what I said about payday loans and other high-cost, small-dollar loans? The federal government created Community Development Financial Institutions to bring mainstream banking to underserved communities. The Small Dollar Loan Program is a safe alternative to predatory lending. Some of the unsecured loans are for as much as $2,500, there are no prepayment penalties, and your payment history is reported to credit bureaus so you can establish a solid credit history.

THE SMALL BUSINESS ADMINISTRATION

The Small Business Administration (SBA) is a government agency that supports entrepreneurs and small businesses, and it also backs small business loans administered through other lenders, such as banks and credit unions. In addition, there are many other federal, state, and local government agencies that provide loans.

While the SBA spent much of the past few years

disbursing COVID-19 relief grants and Paycheck Protection Program (PPP) loans to small businesses that were adversely affected by the pandemic, the SBA still guarantees billions of dollars every year in 7(a) loans to small businesses. The SBA also provides resources, such as counseling and training, to assist new and small businesses. Since 2018, the Small Business Administration has had subcenters at sixteen Historically Black Colleges and Universities around the country to inspire Black entrepreneurs as well as provide business counseling and training services to aspiring Black entrepreneurs.

CREDIT UNIONS AND ALUMNI ASSOCIATIONS

Credit unions are a good option for seed money. One of my first business loans came from a credit union. Your alumni association or place of worship may have a credit union, as they are usually started by people who work together, pray together, know each other well, or have some other factors in common. Credit unions have shown better repayment rates than traditional banks.

President Franklin D. Roosevelt authorized credit unions with the Federal Credit Union Act in 1934 to promote thriftiness during the Great Depression. What I like about them is that they are nonprofit organizations and are owned by the people who are investing in them and are served by them and not by a few, select shareholders. We want to keep the emphasis on the people who are investing, not just the people served.

That's why they typically have lower interest rates on loans and higher interest rates on savings accounts.

CHURCHES

Places of worship are good loan sources, particularly if you or a relative is a longtime member. Many students have been able to go off to college because Sister Williams or Brother Jackson passed the plate around.

A few years ago, Alfred Street Baptist Church, which was founded in 1803 in Alexandria, Virginia, made a $100,000 gift to Howard University, which paid off the debts of thirty-four students who owed the university anywhere from $100 to more than $3,000.[5] Mya Thompson, a senior at the time, took out student loans, received grants and a need-based scholarship, and was working at a 911 call center to attend college and support her young son. It still wasn't enough—until the church stepped in.

INVESTMENT CLUBS

Typically, these clubs comprise individuals who have formed a group to pool their money for investment purposes. However, some clubs also make small business loans.

In 2008, a group of citizens in Port Townsend, Washington, formed the Local Investing Opportunities Network (LION) to create "greater economic self-sufficiency, job growth, economic development, and a dollar-multiplier effect whereby a dollar kept within the community can be spent many times over for a far greater benefit than a dollar invested away from our community."[6] With more than seventy LION members, the group had invested more than $10.5 million in the Port Townsend community by 2021.[7]

There are dozens of investment clubs in cities such as Seattle; Portland, Oregon; Madison, Wisconsin; and New York. You can find them on the Internet and ask them to send you information about what they're doing and looking for in investments.

FRATERNITIES AND SORORITIES

When I was an undergrad, I secured a $250 loan from the graduate chapter of my fraternity, Alpha Phi Alpha, to pay for a room in my college dormitory. In addition, the Flint, Michigan, chapter of the NAACP had a credit union. The manager, Edgar G. Holt, agreed to loan me $150 for tuition. The cost of room, board, and tuition is much more today, of course, but there are good alternatives for funding out there, and tapping into your fraternity's or sorority's local chapter or foundation might be one of them.

VENTURE CAPITALISTS

Venture capitalists are a great alternative resource. They take a risk on something and invest their money on the concept during its initial stages.

ANGEL INVESTORS

Also known as seed investors, angel investors are successful entrepreneurs who provide start-up capital in exchange for equity in a business that they believe has great potential. Think of Mark Cuban, Daymond John, and Kevin O'Leary (aka, "Mr. Wonderful") on the hit reality TV show *Shark Tank*.

You want to identify an angel investor who is willing not only to write you a check but to mentor you, someone who has knowledge and familiarity with your industry and can help you network with other people to make your start-up successful. Depending on what you want to do, you might need someone who can show you the ropes in production, distribution, and retail and online sales. A quick Google search for angel investors will provide you with dozens of lists of the most successful angels who have invested millions of dollars into young companies.

CROWDFUNDING

Crowdfunding websites such as GoFundMe, Kickstarter, and Indiegogo have become increasingly popular. In fact, Kickstarter had successfully funded more than 200,000 projects, totaling more than $6 billion, by 2021. That money came from more than twenty million investors. Basically, a start-up company sets up an online account and explains their venture, and various people can donate small amounts until the desired goal has been reached.

FOUNDATIONS

Foundations distribute loans and grants and have become big players in the entrepreneurship industry. Foundations are nonprofit corporations or charitable trusts that make grants to organizations, institutions, and individuals for charitable causes such as education, health, culture, and religion. The trick is to think holistically and brainstorm ways to ensure that your effort meets the concerns of a particular community.

For example, let's say that you want to open a barbershop on a street that's pockmarked with dilapidated buildings. Here's what you do: Meet with officials at the nearby university and explain that you'd like to open a barbershop in the area, but it can't happen unless certain structures are demolished. If the university wants to see improvements in the surrounding community (and I assure you, it does), it might write a grant to a specific foundation. Before you know it, your goal has been achieved.

In 2021, the Atlanta Wealth Building Initiative launched a campaign to help one thousand Black-owned businesses either hire their first employee or offer living wages to their current employees. According to the group, 96 percent of the Black-owned businesses in the city had no paid employees (compared to 72 percent for white-owned businesses), meaning these businesses were getting by as one-man shops run solely by the entrepreneur who started them.[8]

While federal grants such as PPP went quickly, county and state governments are still offering grants to help small businesses recover from the COVID-19 pandemic. If your small business was just getting off the ground and was adversely affected, you should explore funding that might be available.

SPECIALTY LOANS

Myriad programs are designed to finance businesses run by women and military veterans or to provide incentives for companies to hire them. For instance, the federal government has been known to offer up to $5,000 to businesses that hire veterans. There are even incentives offered to entrepreneurs who were formerly incarcerated or workers who were laid off for five years or more.

There are also tax abatements, interest-free loans, and loan forgiveness for businesses that satisfy some very specific parameters. For example, you can get zero-interest loans if you open your business in a certain zip code where development and revitalization plans are underway. The US Department of Agriculture awards millions of dollars in loans and grants every year through its Rural Development program, which funds rural businesses and co-ops that create quality jobs in rural areas. You can find additional information about these loans on the US Department of Agriculture website or a local USDA office.

SOU-SOUS

Certain ethnic groups, such as Nigerians, Koreans, and West Indians, create sou-sous. The concept of the sou-sou—which is said to have originated in West Africa—remains popular among people from the Caribbean. A sou-sou is a savings arrangement in which members of the group pool an equal amount of money for a set period of time, ranging from weeks, months, a year, and so on. During each rotation, one person gets a "hand," which represents the total amount of group money for that period. The sou-sou keeps doing rotations until everyone in the group has had a turn and has received the full lump sum of his or her hand at least once. It's not unusual for the person who created a sou-sou to take a "cut" from each hand as a fee for administering the sou-sou.

Of course, some argue that it's easier and safer just to keep saving and achieve the same lump-sum effect, especially if the dealer is taking a cut (or Bernie Madoff is running the sou-sou). Another drawback in many sou-sous is that you're not drawing interest on your money. However, if you're the second in line to receive a lump sum, and the number of people involved is very large, then you may have the equivalent of thousands or tens of thousands of dollars that could take you years to save on your own. Many people use sou-sous to start businesses, buy homes, invest in property, and make other significant purchases.

SMALL BUSINESS INCENTIVES

Many cities spur development by establishing special programs with small business incentives, such as Invest Atlanta and Invest Detroit. There are other programs like these across the United States. Either on your own or, hopefully, with the help of hired, seasoned professionals such as a CPA or banker, explore the different programs that exist in almost every city to help new, inexperienced entrepreneurs. They're out there, but without professional help, you may have to know somebody who knows somebody—and hope you get to the right person.

If you have the money, it's best to hire financial professionals to help you navigate the web of potential funding sources. If you can't afford that right now, then I recommend two do-it-yourself resources—the Service Corps of Retired Executives (SCORE), which provides free small business mentoring advice, and your local public library. If you can find one, a business branch of the library is even better. However, as soon as you have the financial wherewithal to do so, I strongly advise you to hire a professional matchmaker to whom you can delegate this important and complex task.

TRADITIONAL BANK LOANS

No matter how many doors get closed in your face, you must keep going. Seek and you shall find. Perhaps your business down payment is just around the corner. If not, maybe it's in your best interest to pull out a larger net and catch a bigger fish, as in an actual bank loan. This is atypical the first time out, but it does happen in certain circumstances. Depending on the scale of the enterprise, a traditional bank loan might be necessary either to launch or expand your business.

But as you prepare to move forward, don't lose sight of one important fact—banks are not in the business of losing money.

Your banker and the bank he or she represents are conservative by nature. If your banker wasn't conservative when hired, then he or she will become conservative very quickly, or that banker won't be employed for long. All a bank does is take Ms. Jones's money and then charge you between 7 to 10 percent interest to borrow it. Your repayment of the loan allows the bank to give Ms. Jones back her 1 or 2 percent interest, use the remainder to pay employee salaries and other operating costs, and turn a profit for the shareholders.

If you plan to go this route, make sure you have a job first. And make sure you keep it long enough to save money and develop a good relationship with the banker. Tell your banker that you're working and want to grow your savings account. Explain that one day you hope to go into business for yourself. A year later, when your banker has seen you consistently saving money every month—even if it's in increments of $30, $50, or $100—and maintaining a credit card debt that is zero or very low, you will have his or her attention. If you're paying off your card balance every month, so you're not paying any interest, not only have you become a regular customer, but your banker will also know that you're a good manager of your resources, no matter how limited they are.

BUSINESS PLANS AND SWOT ANALYSES

Whether you want to borrow $100 or $100 million, the first thing a lending institution will look at is your financial well-being; your credit score; the status of your student loans;

the balances of your credit cards, mortgage or rent, and car payments; and your debt-to-income ratio. If that's in good shape, congratulations! You can now hop on the highway to entrepreneurship.

But first you'll need a solid business plan. You cannot request a bank loan without one. I tell students that a business plan is the bedrock of any good business, but they shouldn't worry if they don't reach their goals immediately. After one hundred and twenty days, some businesses aren't anywhere near their initial business plan projections. The important thing is to establish one. I always urge my students to map out a five-year business plan without focusing too much on cash flow. I'm more interested in the plan and the SWOT analysis (Strengths, Weaknesses, Opportunities, and Threats).

The business plan and SWOT are critical. And like the funding, they're not difficult to establish. All business conferences have trained individuals available to assist you with your business plan and help you refine your SWOT analysis. Once completed, you can approach a bank with confidence and a clear understanding of your direction, despite your inexperience.

PUTTING IT ALL TOGETHER

When I first took out that student loan to cover my equity stake in our McDonald's franchise, it felt like a breeze. However, the completed transaction still involved a bank loan and personal guarantee on the part of the entrepreneur. The Small Business Administration (SBA) guaranteed our first loan, but we had to take out a $100,000 loan to give to McDonald's. We gave the bank $25,000, and the bank had exposure for the remainder. We got a guarantee from the SBA that it would cover 90 percent of the loan if we defaulted. In our case, that guarantee reduced the bank's liability exposure to less than 10 percent.

Fortunately for us, our banker had worked at the SBA and had secured an SBA-backed loan at 3 percent interest. Those we were dealing with at McDonald's corporate headquarters couldn't believe we had gotten such a low interest rate.

I'll never forget the day we strolled into the bank—a trio of ambitious, young Black men, all under the age of thirty— ready to wheel and deal with the big fellas. We felt invincible. My partner, Ray Snowden, a PhD candidate, had written out an agenda for the meeting. Our banker, Aubrey Lee, was deeply impressed by our level of professionalism and organization.

When the loan interview ended, Lee said to us, "I'd like to talk to you without your accountant." After our accountant left, he remarked, "You three brothers have a lot of education, but you don't know a darned thing about business. I'm going to give you three things you must do." He then listed the following:

1. Stay in your business. Be there every day.

2. Don't get involved in charitable giving to numerous community organizations right away. You can do that later.

3. For God's sake, don't buy a Cadillac. Get a Chevrolet, drive it, and save your money. I want you to pay this loan back.

We followed his advice to the letter. But my journey into

the land of loans was far from over. In between the student loan I had used to cover my share of our McDonald's franchise and this SBA-backed loan, I also received a small loan from a credit union. For a while, I was what was considered an absentee co-owner of our franchise. Eventually, McDonald's gave me an ultimatum. I was told to be on-site full time or relinquish my stake in the partnership. In order to meet this demand, I had to move from Cleveland to Detroit immediately. The Mount Sinai Credit Union saved the day with a loan for my moving expenses.

I sought out the local bandwagon again when my partners and I came up with the idea for Vitec Automotive. It was 1997, and we wanted to build a plant that would manufacture plastic fuel tanks, a revolutionary concept at the time. Up until the 1970s, cars had steel bumpers. Back then, gas tanks used in cars and trucks also were constructed of steel. Gas is highly combustible and steel tanks were considered about the only thing durable enough to prevent explosions.

But we were more focused on newer, more resistant plastic tanks. They were destined to become a game changer. We believed in them and wanted to take part in the shift that would soon take place within the auto industry. We located a company in Michigan named Walbrough, which had been building plastic gas tanks for lawn mowers and snowblowers. They were interested in shifting to plastic gas tanks for cars and trucks as well. They felt they could transition into this new enterprise more quickly as part of a minority joint venture because they assumed this affiliation would also make them

a more attractive supplier to original equipment manufac-
turers (OEMs) such as Ford, Chrysler, and General Motors.
However, that's when the door slammed shut. Not a single
bank in Detroit wanted to finance our deal. At least one banker
confided in me that the problem with our deal was that it hit
on all four "New Ps":

- New Process: manufacturing plastic fuel tanks

- New Product: the plastic fuel tanks themselves

- New Plant: we needed to construct an entirely new
  manufacturing facility to build the tanks.

- New People: code for Black folk as the primary employees
  building the fuel tanks.

According to the banker, in order to be an attractive loan
candidate, we should not have had more than two of the four
Ps. But we refused to give up. Our attorney connected with a
Chicago-based financial broker and made him part of our team.
This guy was a dynamo who shopped our plastics concept all
over the country. We got six offers and ended up going with
Bank of America out of Chicago.

Think about it: we had the same deal, same location, and
same people on our team, but because we hired this finance
guru who knew the full breadth of our options, we were able to
get the deal done. The moral of this story is, there is no sense
sitting around moaning and groaning about what you cannot
do. While you're complaining that you can't make it work,
someone else has caught the ball and carried it to the finish
line. As an entrepreneur, you have to make it happen. You have

to try. You have to keep going. Persistence is its own form of capital when it comes to seeking and obtaining financing.

Many of the world's most famous businesspeople failed before they succeeded. Soichiro Honda tried to sell auto parts he'd created to Toyota, but he was quickly rejected. What did he do? He invented a small two-stroke engine and founded Honda Motor Company. Milton Hershey had two candy stores fail before he created the world's most famous candy bar. And at least twelve major publishing houses rejected J. K. Rowling's manuscript, telling her that nobody would want to read about wizards and witches. *Harry Potter and the Sorcerer's Stone* sold 107 million copies worldwide. As Nelson Mandela famously said, "It always seems impossible until it is done."

Here's some real talk:

- Start small, learn, lose, go down, get back up, and learn some more. In the corporate world, there is the concept of the tone at the top. The CEO and other members of the C-suite who drive management create a company's culture, values, and work ethic. When we started Vitec, I was the primary shareholder. Therefore, I stayed off payroll for three years. In doing so, I was sending a message to our team that if I'm not getting paid, we must manage this company as if we're all here running on empty.

- Ignore old-school advice that's preventing you from experiencing a new-school paradigm. Only a few years ago, Black folks would say, "Don't you quit that good job to go into no business." Similarly, young people who had just graduated from college and were starting their careers would hear, "Why don't you go get a steady job? That's what you went to school for. And for God's sake, don't quit and go chasing some foolish pipe dream." If you risk nothing, then you risk everything.

- It's OK to resign from your daily nine-to-five hustle, but please pace yourself. Don't suddenly quit your job just because you heard about a new pizza franchise coming to town. Start stashing away money now, read, do your due diligence, network, build relationships, and work or volunteer in the kind of business you want to own.

- Finance is an ongoing process. As I mentioned earlier, once you secure it, you're still not home free. You have to make sacrifices, and one of those sacrifices is often receiving no salary for a while. This act communicates nonverbally to the entire C-suite and all the managers in your firm that you want to see every penny that goes into this business. I stayed off the payroll for several years for every new company I started. Fortunately, every time I've done so, those ventures have worked out.

- Pay off debts and don't overinvest. As an investor, I'm cautious. I don't invest in things that I don't understand, and I don't invest more money than I can afford to lose. I try to keep my personal, long-term debt at zero or below.

- Attend business conferences and seminars. Whenever and wherever people are talking, you should be there, networking and forming relationships. After all, this is your dream. You have to nurture it to bring it to life.

- Donate, donate, donate! The money you donate not only helps others but also comes back to you. I am a cheerful giver. I give away more than half a million dollars every year to educational and charitable organizations and nonprofits, with a special emphasis on Black groups. This reflects my values.

- Reek of financial conservatism. This means your brief-case, your clothing, and your car. If necessary, borrow your neighbor's car, but do not arrive at a bank, agency, credit union, or any other potential loan office in your BMW, wearing a $9,000 suit, dripping in jewelry, and toting a Gucci handbag. Represent a lifestyle of reason-ableness. Whether you're a billionaire or a thousan-daire, a lifestyle of reasonableness through your physical appearance conveys to your banker your reasonableness with your resources. It helps your banker to understand that you're a good money manager. If you're flashy, your banker will think, *It looks like you already have money. You don't need any from me.*

- Stay away from social media broadcasts and posts that have the potential to put your career in jeopardy. By now, I'm sure you've heard horror stories about people losing jobs because of something they posted on social media, usually Twitter or Facebook, that embar-rasses their company. This conflict occurs at all levels, from waitresses who have made racist comments or badmouthed their employer to vice presidents who have plastered remarks on social media that conflict with the corporation's values. It's common knowledge that companies check social media before making job offers. What would stop an institution from doing the same thing when it's considering you for a loan?

- Savings is the name of the game. The simple act of saving, as my dear friend Ray Snowden taught me, is one of the keys to creating the collateral necessary to secure loans and build wealth. Other keys are saving consistently, constantly keeping track of your spending, exercising discipline, maintaining balance, and being able to distinguish between wants and needs. Remember that a bargain isn't a bargain unless it's something you truly need. Don't buy something just because it's on sale.

- Use your wealth to set a positive financial tone for your family and community. The Bible states, "A good man leaves an inheritance to his children's children" (Proverbs 13:22 ESV). Aim for wealth that is transferrable and intergenerational. After a head of household dies, the family has to cope with a funeral and the burden of grief. When entrepreneurs don't carefully plan with their accountants and lawyers (especially estate lawyers) on all matters concerning their wills and estate, the impact is even more devastating.

GROUND RULES FOR GETTING STARTED

Since I'm pretty sure you'll be overwhelmed at some point, I'd like to remind you of the old adage, "A fool and his money are soon parted." Think about the numerous entertainers, athletes, and lottery winners who attained wealth and lost it because they didn't follow a few ground rules and learn how to invest. That should light a fire under you for a while and keep you focused.

Black folks aren't broke; but traditionally, some of us have made bad choices. I'd like to remind you once again that wealthy people teach their children to *acquire*; middle-income people teach their children to *sell*; and poor people teach their children to *consume*. It's time to break this cycle. Be the role model, the family member who is successful in securing seed capital for one initial venture, and then continues to build on it for the rest of his or her life.

Most of my current net worth is not from McDonald's by a long shot. However, that's where it was born. Everything I have today originated from that first franchise deal. It was thanks to earnings from the various McDonald's restaurants that we owned that I had $150,000 in savings to provide the collateral I needed to get a $150,000 loan to buy Regal Plastics, a company I acquired much later. That initial loan led to more and more deals.

But I wouldn't have reaped the maximum benefits of that entry-level financing experience if I hadn't developed a lifelong habit of being disciplined, penny-wise, and practical. Everybody in my family knows that my first inclination is not to spend money. I'm a generous brother, but I can be tight as a fist. Generally, I don't buy what I don't need. That makes me the frugal one in my group. I have friends who drive Bentleys and wear $5,000 suits every day. I can afford to live that way, but that's not how I roll. I'm content with a Ford and a nice sweater.

I also avoid the Three Cs:

- **Car:** My granddad always said, "It's OK to own a Cadillac, but you need to park it every night on some land that you own." I've also heard it said, "If you have a Land Rover and also have a landlord, you are a landless fool." Buy a nice, dependable used car. You don't need a new BMW or Mercedes. Remember that new cars depreciate much faster than used ones. In fact, a new car's value decreases between 9 percent and 11 percent—as soon as you drive it off the lot! After a year, it will be worth only about 80 percent of what you paid for it and less than half after five years. Find a nice used car, change the oil, take care of it, and drive it until it won't go anymore.

- **Cell phones:** Cell phones have dramatically changed the way we live. Yes, they've made our lives more convenient. We can use them to call Aunt Edna on the other side of the country without paying long-distance charges, check baseball scores anytime we want, play video games, and watch Netflix, Hulu, and other streaming services right there in the palm our hands. But do you really need a new iPhone every time a new edition comes out? The phones nowadays cost more than $1,000, and there are plenty of traps and hidden costs in the contracts you sign with service providers. Consider these statistics: over the average American's lifetime of 78.5 years, he or she will spend $107,066 on cell phones, Internet, and streaming services.[9] Think about that for a minute. Look at your cell phone, Internet, and streaming expenses and figure out a way to consolidate them.

- **Credit cards:** There's such a thing as "good" debt—think student loans, small-business loans, and mortgages. Abusing department store credit cards, frivolously living beyond your means, and fulfilling wants and not needs via credit cards does not qualify as "good" debt—or as good anything. Take the advice of Jay-Z: "I won't buy it until I can buy it twice."[10] If you can't afford it, you more than likely don't need it. According to a survey by Charles Schwab, 59 percent of Americans live paycheck to paycheck.[11] Another study found that three-quarters of people in households making less than $50,000 a year and two-thirds of those making between $50,000 and $100,000 would have a hard time coming up with $1,000 to cover an unexpected bill.[12] That's because a lot of their money is going to high-interest credit card debt. Don't fall into credit card traps. When someone at an airport offers you a credit card with no interest, make sure you read the fine print they're not telling you about. After a year—or as soon as you miss a payment—that interest is probably going to jump to 24.99 percent or higher. That pair of sneakers you bought for $249 is going end up costing you thousands of dollars over the next seven years.

The Three Cs are the traps created by a pesky little habit I call *retail therapy*. Often, people who feel powerless try to validate themselves with expensive things they can't afford. I don't fault them for wanting to pull themselves up; I just wish they would realize the road to wealth is not paved with debt. One of my business partners and I learned that the hard way. Frankly, it was a lesson for all of us. When we opened our third franchise, I wasn't as financially savvy as I am now, and none of us was the best steward of money. We were young, inexperienced, and had no idea that folks who shell out seed capital often know more about you than you know about yourself.

One day, a helicopter mysteriously appeared over a home one of my partners was building in a ritzy Michigan suburb. As it turned out, it was transporting a couple of "spy" executives from a corporate office of an institution that was considering him for a loan. The problem was that he was spending money on new property at a time when he was knee-deep in debt. His request was swiftly denied.

Don't think you can hide missed bill payments. You can't. Don't assume you can mask your credit woes either. When it comes to your financial history, potential lenders are several steps ahead of you. If there are lingering debts, simply come clean and explain what happened—you were laid off from your job, a parent was sick, and so on. Honesty is the best policy in all endeavors, especially when establishing a reputation as an entrepreneur. Everything you do—every bad move and every good one, every major personal purchase, and every business acquisition—will be weighed.

Again, I've been there. Almost as soon as I became a managing partner in 1999 at MGM Resorts International and in 2007 at the MGM Grand Casino, Detroit, I received a phone call, and, of course, I was expecting it. It was my sweet but overprotective mother. She had just finished reading a newspaper article about my new venture, and boy, was she upset. The idea of her son being affiliated with a casino didn't rest well with her.

"Bill, don't do it," she warned. "That's tainted money."

I smiled. But this time I mustered up a response.

"Don't worry, Ma' Dear," I said. "The only time money is tainted is when there tain't enough of it!"

* * *

Surviving the Shift

In the post-pandemic business world, and after the murder of George Floyd heightened awareness about social justice around the world, the US government, financial institutions, and other agencies are finally making an attempt to help Black entrepreneurs and minority-owned businesses thrive. After so many decades of inequality, Americans are beginning to realize that a strong Black and Latino entrepreneur class only strengthens our society as a whole.

As you might know, Black-owned businesses were hit especially hard during the COVID-19 pandemic. According to a recent Stanford University report, between February 2020 to April 2020, there was a 41 percent decrease in the number of Black-owned businesses in the United States.[13]

Blacks and other people of color are behind the eight ball when it comes to starting a business. Another study by the Federal Reserve Bank of New York found that fewer than one in four Black-owned employer firms has a recent borrowing relationship with a bank.[14] It wasn't that Black business owners weren't applying for bank loans as much as white business owners; it's that they were still being turned away by the traditional financial institutions. The report noted that among Black employer firms, 37.9 percent reported being discouraged, compared to 12.7 percent of white-owned firms.[15] Those minority business owners who tried to acquire funding were often met with tedious applications, delays, and, worse, smaller loan amounts and higher interest rates than white borrowers.

"There have been barriers based on race that have kept Black people from opportunity to achieve economic stability, mobility, and prosperity for years," said Phillip Gaskin, vice president of entrepreneurship at the Kauffman Foundation. "Most of these systems were developed long ago, but we're dealing with them still today. If policies aren't designed from the bottom up and inclusively, with the right listening and understanding, then we're going to continue to make mistakes."[16]

David M. Walker, the CEO of StarWalker Industries in Atlanta, knows this dilemma all too well. Not long ago, he went searching for funding for his closed-loop bottled water recycling plant. He found a fund that focused on exactly what he was trying to do. So Walker tried to find a connection on the fund's board, someone who might help grease the wheels. But when he looked through pictures of people on the fund's board of directors, he couldn't find someone who looked like him. All of them were white.

"This fund had about eighty people and not one Black person in it," Walker said. "I looked up and down, scrolling through LinkedIn to find someone that looked like me or [who was] Hispanic. Something, right? And you can't find anybody in that space of funding."[17]

Blount McCormick, president and owner of an Ohio-based travel management company, said her company's revenue dropped 70 percent during the pandemic, from about $37 million in 2019 to $10 million in 2020, as people stayed home and quit traveling.[18] Inexplicably, a banker told her to max out her credit cards to keep her firm afloat. When it was time for her to apply for a Paycheck Protection Program (PPP) loan from the federal government, she opted to go to a private lender.

"Banking while Black is very difficult, and that happens and it's not surprising, unfortunately. So I found a private lender," she told *Fortune*.[19]

The good news, ladies and gentlemen, is that help is on the way. Through private investors, grants, and loans, Black business owners are finding alternative ways to seed their start-ups. According to *Fortune*,

> *There continue to be efforts to support Black businesses and entrepreneurs, including Amazon's announcement of its Black Business Accelerator, a $150 million commitment over four years to provide financial support and mentorship. Wall Street titan Goldman Sachs also committed $10 billion in direct investment for Black women's education, small business, and employment over the next ten years with its One Million Black Women initiative.[20]*

So how might you fund your new business venture in the COVID-19 world or restart the one that might have been adversely affected by the pandemic? As I mentioned earlier, there are myriad ways to find money besides traditional banks and other financial institutions, including the following options.

Small Business Term Loans

In addition to the conventional brick-and-mortar banks that we all know, there are various online lenders that fund small business start-ups. Look for the best options on sites such as fundinghero.com and nerdwallet.com. Some of the lenders have minimum requirements in monthly revenue and how long you've been in business, but others are more flexible. You can borrow anywhere from $5,000 to $6 million, but don't take more than you need. Remember that you're going to be paying 6 percent interest or more over the term of the loan, and that money is going to add up. Depending on how much you borrow, you'll be required to pay it back in as little as six months, or a couple of years if you need more money. Unlike those PPP loans that Uncle Sam handed out so freely, you're going to have to pay this money back!

BUSINESS LINE OF CREDIT

I prefer a business line of credit to a business term loan because it allows a business owner to borrow up to a set limit. For example, my company's credit line might be $25,000, but if I use only $2,000 in the first month, I'm only paying interest on that lesser amount. If you don't use the line of credit, you don't have to make payments and interest doesn't accrue. On the other hand, once you take out a business loan, you're required to make payments and pay interest on the entire loan, whether you've used the money or not. Like a credit card, most lines of credit allow you to make smaller monthly payments or to pay the entire balance back all at once. If you're in a financial position to pay the total balance, do it!

Recently, there have been several venture capitalist firms that are geared to target minority entrepreneurs.

BACKSTAGE CAPITAL

Arlan Hamilton, a forty-year-old Black woman, is the founder and managing partner of Backstage Capital. She built the venture capital fund from the ground up—while she was homeless! Founded in 2015, Backstage Capital has raised more than $15 million and invested in 170 start-up companies led by what she calls underestimated founders— women, people of color, and those who are LGBTQ+. Every year, the group invests in dozens of companies operating in various sectors and multiple regions of the country. You can be a sole proprietor or have multiple employees. Backstage Capital says the majority of its initial investments range from $25,000 to $100,000.

What I really like about Backstage Capital is that they don't simply write entrepreneurs a check and then wait for a return on investment. Instead, they have dozens of mentors with diverse experience, skills, and talents to help young entrepreneurs launch their businesses. They include executives from Amazon, Mashable, Slack, Reddit, and Booz Allen Hamilton. You can learn more about Backstage Capital and obtain its application for funding at backstagecapital.com.

HARLEM CAPITAL PARTNERS

As you probably guessed, Harlem Capital is a New York City–based venture capital firm with a "mission to change the face of entrepreneurship by investing in 1,000 diverse founders over the next 20 years." Harlem Capital has already invested in start-ups such as Beauty Bakerie, an organic cosmetics producer that markets to women of color, and Blavity, a media platform that focuses on Black millennials.

Managing partners Henri Pierre-Jacques and Jarrid Tingle founded Harlem Capital in 2015. They attended Harvard Business School together and wanted to focus on investing in entrepreneurs who were underserved by traditional fundraising. They raised $40 million in their first venture-capital fund in 2019, and then another $134 million—in just five months—in March 2021. Apple and PayPal wrote two of the second fund's anchor checks. Harlem Capital said 61 percent of its Fund I portfolio companies are led by Black or Latino executives; 43 percent are led exclusively by women.[21]

Pierre-Jacques and Tingle told *Forbes* that they want to build the "Motown of VC" and help create the most Black and Latino millionaires ever. That's music to my ears, brothers.[22]

Remember this more than anything else: if you don't have enough money in the bank, find creative ways to make it. One of the best success stories in fast-food history involves two childhood friends from Georgia who were crazy enough to launch a chicken finger business in the heart of Chick-fil-A country.

Zach McLeroy and Tony Townley had known each other

since the fifth grade. When McLeroy graduated from high school, his parents sat him down and explained that they would love for him to go to college. No one in his family had ever gone, but, unfortunately, they couldn't afford to send him. So McLeroy paid his own way through the University of Georgia. He purchased carpet remnants from mills in Dalton, Georgia, and sold them to college students living in dorm rooms. He bought Christmas trees in North Carolina and sold them in Georgia.

When they decided to open their first chicken restaurant in Statesboro, Georgia, McLeroy sold his drums to help raise the money. McLeroy and Townley each pitched in $8,000, and they took out a bank loan to pay for their building. They made $350,000 in sales in the first year.[23] In 2020, Zaxby's had more than nine hundred restaurants in seventeen states. The chain was so successful that Goldman Sachs acquired a significant stake in the company. If those dudes can make billions off chicken fingers, the sky's the limit for you!

CHAPTER 5

PRINCIPLE 4:
Build Good Relationships

*Lots of people want to ride with you in the limo,
but who you want is someone who will
take the bus with you when the limo breaks down.*
—Oprah Winfrey

WHENEVER A DEAL is about to collapse, I turn to a guy known for his quick thinking and unorthodox theories. I call him Larry "Out of the Box" Crawford. He's a Detroit area dentist-turned-entrepreneur whose investment ideas are so unusual they often defy reason.

He's also one of the most respected members of my squad. My squad—Larry Crawford, Ron Hall, Alex Parrish, Dennis Archer, Roy Roberts, Don Snider, Ray Snowden, Gordon Follmer, Thomas Dortch Jr., and Roosevelt Adams—consists of close friends with whom I share interests, values, and goals. I call them my squad, but we're actually more like a tribe in a communal village. We have a strong bond and a lifelong loyalty. We have depended on one another, rescued one another, and taught one another a thing or two about etiquette, history, ethics, and business.

Where did I get my keen understanding of the luxury car industry? I got that from Hall, the president and CEO of Bridgewater Interiors, an automotive interiors manufacturing firm. Politics? That's from Archer, the former mayor of Detroit, of course. Snider and Crawford showed me how to network. Snowden taught me to save. Follmer inspired me to believe there's a solution to every problem. Adams, Dortch, Roberts, and Parrish? They're natural diplomats who helped me expand my vision and grow as a civic leader.

Good relationships are like that. When they are carefully nurtured and cultivated like your grandmama's favorite houseplant, they can be more valuable than your weight in diamonds. In many ways, a trusted comrade is like having access to a secret code. He or she can magically open doors. Here's why: the people you kick it with today—your right-hand man on the basketball court or your buddies from the dorm—could be part of your network, alliance, or political connections tomorrow. They could be your future references, referral sources, and business leads. They are the special path that you have already paved.

Just look at it this way: let's say you have a degree in marketing and your college roommate works in the human resources department at a Fortune 500 company. If you need a job, who are you going to call? Then there's your former biology lab partner. Pretend, for a minute, that he's now part owner of a fabulous, five-star hotel. What if I told you that you'd get cool points and your business worth would increase exponentially every time you and this brother were seen together?

Not convinced? Well, let me break it down further.

There was once a rich investor in New York whom I'll call Joseph Thompson (not his real name). During the Great Depression, he lost everything. So, he decided to reach out to his friend, John D. Rockefeller. Because he had fallen so low on the social totem pole, Thompson was kind of worried that Rockefeller wouldn't bother to take his call. He phoned his office anyway and told his secretary that he wanted to invite Rockefeller to lunch.

Rockefeller accepted and agreed to meet with Thompson the following day. As the two strolled down Wall Street to Rockefeller's private club, heads turned and people began to whisper: "That's Joseph Thompson with John D. Rockefeller, but isn't Thompson flat broke? I don't know, that's Rockefeller with him. Rockefeller always knows what's going on."

Both men entered the club, and Rockefeller was shown to his private table. The buzz continued among those sitting around them. Immediately, Rockefeller excused himself to go wash his hands. At that moment, several people of wealth and influence approached Thompson and began showering him with requests to meet to discuss potential business deals. When Rockefeller returned and asked Thompson what he wanted to talk about, all Thompson could do was smile.

"Don't worry," he said. "I have it all taken care of."

We've all heard of guilt by association. Well, this was a case of success by association. When the other club members saw Thompson with Rockefeller, they automatically assumed that he was someone worth getting to know. This has often been referred to as "birds of a feather flock together," which is one of the oldest and most common expressions ever uttered. It's also one of the truest. We are judged by the company we keep, in good ways and not-so-good ways. As your grandparents probably once told you, "Show me your friends, and I'll show you your future."

FINDING FRIENDS WHO'LL SHAPE YOUR FUTURE

During my early high school years of goofing off and thinking little of myself, I stuck with the crowd of underachievers who fit my low self-image. And doesn't everyone? What straight-A students do you know who perpetually hang around with kids who are failing or getting into fights after class? Successful students know that if they set foot on that crooked path, before long they'll be on a fast train to nowhere. I often tell young people that if you see nine broke brothers on a corner, don't join them. If you do, there will be ten broke brothers. Believe me, if you tell me who your five closest friends are, I can tell you where you're going to be in five to ten years. Your relationships shape you, define you, and help carve out your future.

How do you find and develop the best relationships? There are at least three approaches.

GET TO KNOW PEOPLE WHO SHARE YOUR VALUES

There are the people who will become your closest friends, your road dogs, those special buddies who remain in your life forever. Sometimes you encounter them in childhood or high school. For me, it was college. I had a terrific roommate named Dennis Archer, and we connected like blood brothers. By then, I was no longer the insecure guy who ate lunch under the stairwell and grumbled about school. So of course, I gravitated to those who shared my newfound interests. Dennis and I both loved books, deep conversations, and—well, how can I put this? We also had the same budget, which was no budget at all. We were poor dudes in a dorm that didn't serve food. A lasting bond was formed as we ate Spam, sardines, and other canned meat together. Obviously, those were the days. Because of them, Dennis and I have a priceless, lifelong camaraderie. Neither of us had any idea that he would one day become the mayor of Detroit.

Many of the most successful businesses in the world were the creations of lifelong friends or college classmates. Apple founders Steve Jobs and Steve Wozniak met when Jobs was fifteen or sixteen years old and Wozniak was about twenty or twenty-one, while both were working at a Hewlett-Packard factory. Before Microsoft became a $2 trillion business, Paul

Allen and Bill Gates met as teenagers in the late 1960s at Lakeside School in Seattle, when Gates was in eighth grade and Allen was in tenth grade. Likewise, Ben Cohen and Jerry Greenfield met while running around the track in seventh grade. They reunited in New York after school, then moved to Vermont to create the world's most famous ice cream.

CREATE A DOMINO EFFECT

As you and your friends mature, you will begin to make referrals for one another and offer leads to jobs. Possibly, these leads will have a cumulative effect. One friend in a good position will hire one, then another. Along the way, the squad will begin to swap investment ideas and/or make plans to pursue a business partnership. Just like tipping dominos, you will push one another forward. If I hadn't had a significant relationship with Detroit Urban League president Dr. Francis A. Kornegay, my meeting with Henry Ford might not have taken place. Dr. Kornegay, my longtime mentor, took me to Henry Ford and said, "Henry, this is my boy. He has a bunch of those McDonald's stands, and he wants to be a car dealer." This meeting with Ford was a life-changing experience that led to my ownership of Regal Plastics.

While there's a fine line when it comes to friends hiring friends, and you have to weigh the pros and cons of those situations, your friends can provide support and networking opportunities during job hunts. Your friends might know people who work in the sector you're interested in breaking into, and they might be able to introduce you to them and set up job shadowing them to give you a better idea of what the job actually involves. If nothing else, your friend can introduce you to people in the industry who might be willing to answer your questions and offer good advice. A job search can be lonely so don't be afraid to turn to your friends, who might be gold mines in terms of connections and networking. Once you've landed your dream job, you can return the favor and help someone else in need of employment.

GET IN THE MIX

Being part of the mix is essential because it puts you where you need to be to meet those people you want to know. You have to belong to something, be it a sorority, fraternity, alumni organization, church, community group, or a nonprofit. Get involved. Volunteer. Everyone has a skill or an activity they enjoy. Figure out what that activity is for you. But before you do, make sure you know how to pace yourself and manage your expectations. When you volunteer for political campaigns, don't expect to become a director the first time around. Stay humble and focused on serving. That's the real reason you're there. (Of course, getting in the mix is part of it, too, but service always comes first.)

Please remember this: there's no mixing without giving, sharing, and doing your best. Pass out flyers, knock on doors, do grunt work. If you're introverted, accept assignments that don't require face-to-face interaction, such as making phone calls and reading from a script. Or you can volunteer to do research. In short, when you volunteer for campaigns, or for anything, find the right fit and be driven by passion without expecting glory. Along the way, something good is bound to happen, often when you're not anticipating it. This is one of the things that fuels my own passion for volunteerism. After I throw myself wholeheartedly into an important cause, someone will suddenly give me a much-needed push or surprise me by opening a door that advances my career.

FILLING ROLES IN YOUR SQUAD

My current team of confidantes is a direct result of the relationships and networks I deliberately nourished. As I slowly climbed the ladder to success, I met some incredible people who have helped spirit me toward my goals. They are the people I believe in and the people who believe in me. But that type of camaraderie doesn't bloom overnight. An overnight or fly-by-night connection is simply an acquaintance, someone you speak to on campus, make small talk with about the game, or with whom you have pleasant surface relationships. The long-term, genuine bonds are the ones you forge over a period of time with individuals with whom you have a more personal connection. You can share information, secrets, dreams, and even money.

A billionaire friend of mine once put it this way: "Who would you give or loan a couple thousand dollars? That's your core guy." If there is someone you wouldn't hesitate to hand a sizable amount of money to, you have exited the realm of being an acquaintance and entered the territory of being a dear friend.

As I've said, I call friends who fit in this category my "squad." This is the tightest circle imaginable, the brothers with whom you share lighthearted moments, conduct business, and discuss situations and details you would be embarrassed to share with anyone else. Within the squad, you can feel vulnerable. While interacting with them, you can let down defensive barriers and peel off whatever mask you might be wearing. Each of them is "a brother from another mother," and each helps you embrace and maximize your potential. But make no mistake, all our relationships are distinct, and a few are fairly complex. Some are friendships coupled with mentorships, while others are mentorships or friendships combined with sponsorships. Or they are vertical relationships. Regardless, they all comprise the next level up in relationships.

Let's review the handful of different types of relationships that will likely be represented as you build your squad.

Vertical and Horizontal Relationships

Vertical relationships are friendships with people who are older, wiser, and more experienced. They are often mentors who take you under their wings and show you the ropes. Vertical relationships are like the ones you had with your parents and grandparents or the favorite uncle who taught you how to fish.

Horizontal relationships are the ones you have with your siblings, classmates, and friends. These are your peers, the men and women who are running alongside you.

When developing relationships, especially vertical ones in

which people are more advanced in age or their careers than you are, make sure to acknowledge and show appreciation for their assistance and expertise. Look up to them and respect them. It makes most people feel good to know they are helping others. However, exercise good judgment. Cultivating this feeling in others isn't an open-access pass to becoming needy or greedy.

MENTOR RELATIONSHIPS

Mentorships can take different forms, from verbal encouragement and career guidance to lending financial assistance and helping you improve your diction and professional appearance. When Mark Zuckerberg was in the early days of developing Facebook, he turned to Steve Jobs, who as a young entrepreneur had already changed the world with Apple. Back when Oprah was in the early days of her television career, she went to the famous poet Maya Angelou for direction. J. J. Abrams was the son of TV producers, but he leaned on his idol, Steven Spielberg, when he wanted to make his mark in Hollywood as a young director. Spielberg was a sounding board for Abrams, who became what many are now calling "the Steven Spielberg of his generation." After the Detroit rapper Eminem had been turned down by just about every record label, Dr. Dre heard his demo and signed him to a deal. Eminem paid respect to Dr. Dre in a song: "All I know is you came to me when I was at my lowest. You picked me up, breathed new life in me, I owe my life to you."[1] Later, Eminem paid it forward by mentoring 50 Cent when he was struggling for a break.

SPONSOR RELATIONSHIPS

Sponsorships are about leverage. A sponsor picks up the phone or goes to bat for you on matters and in ways that are critical to your advancement. As a person of influence, a sponsor may put in a word that makes the difference between your admission into a master's program at Columbia University—or not. Once you're accepted, unbeknownst to you, that same sponsor may create a $5,000 scholarship that will help defray tuition costs your first year. A sponsor's role is action-oriented.

It's important to note that sometimes your mentor and sponsor have to be two different people. Oftentimes, the person who mentors you doesn't have the capacity or influence to act as sponsor. Two of my favorite professors were Albert Rogers and James Randall. They guided and pushed me through community college. Francis Kornegay (via Henry Ford II) opened the door to my highly profitable entrance into the automotive industry. Dennis Archer included my name in a list of recommendations he gave to MGM Resorts International as possible casino partners in Detroit. At this point my friend Dennis became my sponsor as well.

Sponsorship has played a role in my ownership of more than one company. So has networking. Early in my career, I was on the equivalent of what felt like ninety-nine different boards. I was a single man, and I didn't want to be poor all my life. I willingly signed up for whatever I thought would help me move forward. While I was serving on the board for Oakwood Hospital in Michigan, I met John Sagan, someone I would meet again when we went to see Henry Ford II with Dr. Kornegay. Based on our work together on the board, Sagan was able to offer Ford a firsthand assessment of my character. That incident was the perfect cocktail of relationships and politics blended together, yielding wonderful results.

NETWORKING IS ESSENTIAL

Back in the day, I used to know a big-time numbers man who was even more successful than my Uncle Paul. He encouraged me and a dentist friend, Larry (the one I call "Out of the Box" Crawford), to invest in a plastics company in Saginaw, Michigan. However, General Motors wouldn't do the deal with my buddy since they didn't know him, and he hadn't been in the plastics industry long enough. On the other hand, I was known. My master networking skills paid off, and I acquired majority ownership in the firm. Later, I was able to make Crawford a Vitec shareholder and appoint him to the board. This is a perfect example of the unpredictable, yet highly fruitful, manner in which relationships can work. It's a symphony of give-and-take based on your ability to follow three steps:

1. Network.

2. Network.

3. Repeat steps 1 and 2

And to all you naysayers who might be reading and furrowing your brows, hear this: I feel you. I know you've heard some unsavory gossip about the networking circuit. I get it.

You think it's brownnosing. You actually believe that getting to know specific people and mingling in certain circles makes you a sellout. You may even be tossing around terms such as "waste of time" or "phony." Well, listen up: nothing could be more off base. You're delusional, and it's time to pull your head out of the sand. There is a golden rule and a rock-hard truth about success: you either *network* or you *don't work*!

So if you didn't get it the first time, I'll say it again: when you get along great with someone and really like him or her, that's your friend. However, it just so happens that three years later, that same friend might end up at Spelman College or Morehouse College as president of the student body. He or she then discovers the college is developing a program for people from urban areas who are entering college in their twenties. Your friend thinks about you. You apply—and get in. You had simply developed a relationship with a person who was going to college, and that relationship bore fruit in an unexpected and wonderful way.

Understand that I'm not suggesting that you enter relationships thinking a person is going to get you what you need. For instance, a friend of mine once told me about a strange encounter she observed during a vacation in Egypt. One of her traveling companions casually mentioned to the others in their tour group that he hoped to make friends with one of the local citizens. He reasoned that if he made a friend, he wouldn't have to pay for a hotel the next time he traveled to the region. The next day, as they were sitting in a restaurant enjoying dinner, an Egyptian gentleman approached the group and welcomed them to his homeland.

My friend said she watched in horror as her traveling companion introduced himself, and then immediately asked the man he had just met if he could stay at his home during future visits. This scene is a nightmarish demonstration of brownnosing at its worst. This is not, I repeat, not networking. It's a crude example of the stereotypical ugly American. It also contradicts my message. Do not confuse networking with being a grabby opportunist. That's the complete opposite of what I'm saying here. In fact, that kind of attitude won't get you anywhere. It's mooching, not networking.

True networking requires you to shift your mental gears. It means you are befriending someone who brings out the best in you. It's a two-way street. It suggests that, if needed, you are willing to extend yourself on this person's behalf and follow one of self-help author Dale Carnegie's chief guidelines: "The only way on Earth to influence the other fellow is to talk about what he wants and show him how to get it."[2]

Now, that's networking at its peak. But it won't occur unless both individuals click. And it won't flow unless both of you remain principled and authentic. When that type of beautiful synergy is present, it's possible for events to unfold organically. There's an African proverb that states, "If you want to go fast, go alone. If you want to go far, go with others." Networking means you're inviting others along for the ride. Because I know it's necessary, I learned to do this as best as I could. In fact, I became pretty good at it. I only wish my close friend, the late Ray Snowden, had become as much of a political animal as I had. Ray thought he'd be awarded more

McDonald's franchises because he had an incredible work ethic and ran a tight operation at his other franchises. His expectations never materialized. Mine did.

The only differences between us were the genuine relationships I cultivated with those at McDonald's who were influencers and decision-makers in the franchise process. Unlike many people, my political acumen came naturally. In college, I was elected to serve on the Interfraternity Council, which consisted of all fifteen fraternities on campus—thirteen white fraternities and the only two Black ones, the Alphas and the Kappas. I recognized early on that if I could get the support of six of the white fraternities and of the two Black fraternities (the latter I had in the bag), I could get anything on my agenda passed. That was my first big experience in navigating the political aspects of life—and I nailed it. Ditto for my daughter, who became president of her senior class at Spelman College with very little effort. I asked her, "Mary, why did you run for president? You're not from Atlanta, and you're not in a sorority."

She replied, "Dad, I just knew there were only about three hundred women I needed to impact in order to win, because most of them don't vote."

I responded, "You had three hundred names?"

"No," she said. "But I had about forty people I knew could impact people." That's how she got her three hundred.

As I listened to my daughter, I smiled just a bit and fought back a desire to laugh. I recognized myself in my child. I realized then and there that she has both the IQ and

EQ (emotional quotient) to navigate relationships and hone political instincts. At an early stage in life, she knows that if she has supporters, she can't fail—at least not completely.

TACKLING TOUGH RELATIONSHIP QUESTIONS

Like anything else in life, there will be speed bumps, challenges, and plenty of questions in your relationships. What follows are some of the questions I've been asked.

How Can You Ensure Certain People Will Benefit from Your Business Concerns?

That's easy. One of my fondest memories involves another one of my longtime mentors, Art Johnson. Art dedicated his life to public service and spent thirty years working for the Detroit NAACP. He focused more on community efforts and public service rather than personal advancement. He was the "Pied Piper" for the NAACP and got me to leave the Urban League to work for them. When I went to work for the Cleveland NAACP, I could call him for advice, which made people think I was smart. Art was sixty years old when I became a comanaging partner in Detroit's MGM Grand. We were able to make him part of the deal. You can't help everyone, but if there are a few people that helped you out along the way, try to make room for them in your new enterprise.

Is It OK to Enter a Business Relationship with Someone You Don't Like Personally?

Yes and no. There are people you may not like but, for pragmatic reasons, might have to collaborate with on a business deal. Generally, this doesn't bother me. However—and this is important—there are some people I would never do business with because of their severe and proven moral and ethical deficits.

The bottom line is, we're not going to like everyone we encounter, no matter how nice we might be. Just remember not to let your emotions get the best of you, and keep in mind that what they might be doing or saying that rubs you the wrong way probably isn't personal. Pick your battles and never let your temper get in the way of a good deal. Nine out of ten times, we're going to do business with people we like and those who have like-minded goals. In those rare instances in which we have to do a deal with someone we can't stand, rise above the hate and be patient. Remember that trust is an essential component, more so than whether you "like" that person. You can deal with people you don't like as long as you can trust them. If you can't trust someone, you should stay away from them, whether you like them or not.

How Do You Avoid Relationships That Compromise Your Integrity?

There's one incident in my entrepreneurial career that answers this question perfectly. I received a call from a regional vice president of McDonald's who told me the corporation was going to reward me with a franchise within a major business district. This deal was going to be a game changer. As I envisioned the nonstop business that would flow through this new site, I thought, *This thing is going to print money.* Later, one of the district's executives called and asked to meet. We met at a restaurant in my lawyer's office building. During our meeting, he began to toss around the word *partnership*. Finally, I asked him flat out if he was asking for a kickback. He acknowledged that he was. I immediately drew our meeting to a close and told him I didn't want to speak with him anymore.

What he was proposing was illegal and went against my business ethics. I had no intention of putting the gaming license that allowed me to be a partner of the MGM Grand Detroit in jeopardy. However, these people would not go away. They approached me several more times, and even my attorney could not get them to be reasonable. They insisted that I "play ball" in order to land the restaurant. Finally, I told them to "take the restaurant and shove it." Next, I had to tell McDonald's that I couldn't accept the new franchise, but I had to couch it in a way that would not make them think I had lost interest. I explained that my circumstances prohibited a new business endeavor. I said I was newly married and my mother-in-law had moved into the home I shared with my wife. All of this was true, but it was not the reason I stepped away. That restaurant did $5 million in sales its first year at a time when the average McDonald's restaurant was earning $2 million annually. But the executive behind that unsavory scheme was eventually fired.

Is It Possible to Get Business Ideas and Deals from a Passing Acquaintance?

Yes! When I was about twenty-six years old, I managed to get one of those $99 student travel deals to Freeport, Bahamas. While I was on the beach, I met a teacher named C. A. Smith who was around thirty-one years old at that time. We struck up a friendship and stayed in touch. I would see him every other winter or summer. By the time I was appointed by President Ronald Reagan to serve as chairman of the African Development Foundation, C. A. Smith had risen to become a member of Parliament in The Bahamas. When the Bahamians were trying to craft a deal on the Caribbean Basin Initiative, I was able to lend a hand. Later, C. A. became the Bahamian ambassador to the United States, under the first President Bush. I was able to help C. A. on some of his initiatives, and he was able to reciprocate and help me with some of mine.

You never know where an accidental encounter will lead you. Stay in touch. Just remember that God puts people in your life for a reason, and He removes them (like the unscrupulous McDonald's executive) for a better reason.

Can a Relationship Save You from Disaster?

Absolutely! I had grown Regal Plastics's revenue from $25 million to $50 million, when suddenly the company hit a brick wall. I didn't have the people or resources I needed to keep business flowing, and the bank demanded that I agree to a personal guarantee or they would call in the loan and put the company into bankruptcy. This was one of the worst episodes of my entrepreneurial career. However, my friends were working feverishly to help me save my business. Art Johnson played the conciliator and, with the help of Ron Hall and my attorney, Alex Parrish, we were able to block that worst-case scenario. They convinced the bank to give me more time to stabilize Regal.

RELATIONSHIPS CREATE AND MAXIMIZE OPPORTUNITIES

Not everyone agrees with me, I'm sure, but I fervently believe in divine order. Fortunately, I have the right squad in place to help things along as well. When I was in my twenties and thirties, whenever I had problems, I would retreat to Ann Arbor, Michigan, and sit in front of the house I had once lived in as a graduate student. I found that setting very meditative. Being there helped me clear my head and reach important decisions.

One Friday night, I came home from working late at McDonald's, and my place in Detroit was in chaos. The police had conducted a drug raid in the wee hours of the morning that led to a fire in the building. The fire department extinguished the blaze, causing a flood in my apartment. It was a wild night. I immediately headed to the steps of my Ann Arbor refuge. I lived two minutes away from Interstate 94, which is the straight route I normally took to get to Ann Arbor. I was going to take my typical drive, get a hot dog along the way, ride around campus, sit in front of my old house, and think. But for some reason, I suddenly decided to take the scenic route down Michigan Avenue.

At that time, Black folks didn't live in that area, known as Dearborn. But given what I'd just experienced at my apartment, I wasn't thinking about demographics. I simply pulled up to Michigan Avenue and Rotunda Drive and saw a sign that said, "Opening. New Apartments and Townhouses, Fairlane East." I made a snap decision to stop in and grab a brochure. After that, I headed to Ann Arbor and bought my hot dog. By then it was around 1:00 p.m., and although I had been up all night, I had to be back to McDonald's by 5:00 p.m. for that evening's shift.

As I drove along, I decided to make one last stop, this time to see a friend who lived in the area. After stepping inside her house, I abruptly announced, "I'm fed up. I'm ready to move."

"Move where?" she asked.

I handed her the brochure. She started laughing and said, "This is Dearborn!"

I said, "Dearborn?" I hadn't even thought about the location. It was 1981, and the place I was interested in renting was a three-bedroom unit that would cost $1,100 a month. That was a sizable amount of money at that time, but I could afford it. It was a very nice area, a quiet gated community equipped with a twenty-four-hour security guard.

The Monday after that, I filled out the application for the apartment. A few days later, I received an odd phone call from a man I had never met. He told me his name was Larry Washington.

"We see that you filled out an application last Friday," he said.

"Mr. Washington," I said, "I don't know you, but I'm not looking for any trouble. I'm not trying to move into Dearborn."

"Calm down," he responded. "We want this place integrated. I've done my research on you, and you used to work for the NAACP in Cleveland."

"Yes, sir," I answered.

He said, "I'm chairman of the NACCP in Detroit, and I want to come by McDonald's in Detroit and talk to you."

When we met in person, he handed me his card. I stared in disbelief. Stamped on the card were the words "Assistant to Henry Ford II, Chairman and CEO." (Bear in mind, this all occurred before my meeting with Ford.) Washington added, "All I want you to do is listen to me. You're in the Republican Party—you're vice chairman in Michigan. If you agree to move to Dearborn, I will put you on the Oakwood Hospital board, and I will put you on any commission or board you want in the city of Dearborn."

Many of Ford Motor Company's top executives sat on the Oakwood Hospital board. Guess what? I moved to Dearborn. This sums up the power of reciprocal relationships and the importance of having a network—particularly one of high caliber. Whenever I read about accomplished individuals, I can't help but notice that many of them aligned themselves with like-minded people, all of whom entertained innovative concepts and ideals. These carefully guarded relationships helped those individuals climb to greater heights.

Thomas Edison traveled the world and associated with his squad—Harvey Firestone, Henry Ford, and Luther

Burbank—in order to maximize his talent. Edison was blessed that he had Firestone, Ford, Burbank, and others who could challenge him and encourage him to widen his intellectual gifts.

Try it, and you'll see what I mean. Gather a group of your most determined friends and set collective and individual goals. Then challenge each other to reach them. Years ago, three Black teens from a crime-ridden community in Newark, New Jersey, did that and more. They made a passionate vow to assist one another in their quests to get out of the hood and make their dreams of becoming doctors a reality. These days, they are known as Dr. George Jenkins, Dr. Sampson Davis, and Dr. Rameck Hunt—a dentist and two physicians who readily acknowledge they were "drawn together for a purpose." Authors of the *New York Times* bestseller *The Pact*, they now create opportunities for others through their nonprofit, The Three Doctors Foundation. They're also on the lecture circuit, visiting schools across the country and speaking about the experiences that gave birth to their careers.

How about you? Can you and your crew stick together and make the same quantum leap? Maintaining relationships is easier than you think. Just be willing to take the time. I keep in touch via phone calls, emails, and text messages. I'm also a prolific reader and pass on—unprompted—information I think people will find valuable. Based on their interests, their current life stage, or significant events that have occurred in their lives, I email links to online articles or a heads-up about an upcoming deal or event.

I do this because I cherish the bonds I have formed. No matter what stage of life I enter or how much money I have amassed, I'm still awed and humbled by all the love and support my relationships have provided. And I find that I'm still reaping the rewards. My connections have helped maintain my reputation. They keep my pride, my honor, and my word alive. Because my network has my back, my businesses have been able to glide into soft landings at times when I thought they would crash. Enterprises I never anticipated have soared beyond my wildest hopes. Struggles that could have ruined me financially have morphed into stories of grandeur and triumph.

And I owe it all to my squad.

* * *

Surviving the Shift

Like just about everything else in the business world, the worldwide COVID-19 pandemic greatly altered the way we network and meet other professionals in our industry. In the past, traditional networking opportunities included face-to-face events such as chamber of commerce meetings, alumni groups, business organizations, job fairs, civic clubs such as Kiwanis and Rotary, trade shows, professional conventions, and happy hours. Those are the places where salespeople and entrepreneurs would gather every week or month to talk shop, develop relationships, interact with customers and coworkers, and plant the seeds for potential deals.

Unfortunately, the pandemic eliminated most of those face-to-face opportunities we had grown accustomed to. Since networking is still an integral part of landing a job, boosting your career, and building relationships in business, where can you now "work the room" to meet as many new people as possible, including those who might one day be your squad? Fortunately, it is now happening in a place you are already very familiar with—the World Wide Web.

Social media platforms such as Twitter, Facebook, TikTok, LinkedIn, and Instagram can be both good and bad in developing your professional career. I'm sure you've been warned about the dangers of posting something foolish on social media. How many times have you read about a celebrity who was "canceled" for something they might have posted on social media? A 2020 study found that 90 percent of employers used social media when evaluating potential hires and 79 percent of human resources professionals had denied a candidate a job because he or she had posted something inappropriate on social media.[3]

It isn't rocket science. Just remember, first and foremost, that what you share on social media portrays who you are as a person. While being a shock jock on Twitter might earn you points with your boys, it's probably going to leave you unemployed after college. Act professionally and don't get too personal. No one wants to read about the beef you might be having with your sister or significant other. Never post hate speech or inappropriate language, pornography, or photographs or videos of alcohol or drug use. Don't get too political. Post only those things that would make your grandmama proud. How you act on social media is a significant part of your personal brand, and it will be weighed as much as your résumé, academic achievements, and work experience by potential employers and companies that might want to do business with you. Wouldn't it be a crying shame if being cool on social media for a brief moment wiped out years of hard work? Trust me, it has happened over and over again. Once you hit send, it's too late to take it back. Someone out there will find it, no matter how long ago it might have been posted.

Despite the dangers of social media, it still plays an important part in your professional development—if it is used correctly and responsibly. LinkedIn, which was founded in a living room in 2002 and sold to Microsoft for $26.2 billion in

2016, calls itself the "world's largest professional network," with more than 810 million members in two hundred countries and territories around the world.[4] During the fourth quarter of the 2021 fiscal year, LinkedIn reported that its sessions had increased 30 percent compared to the previous year.[5] As more and more workers were isolated at home and offices remained closed, would-be employers and employees connected with each other on LinkedIn. It's also a great way for salespeople and entrepreneurs to find prospective customers. It's a wonderful place to post your résumé and references. People who might have worked with you in the past can offer referrals and endorsements. Another thing I like about LinkedIn is that it organizes content on specific industries to keep its users up to date on emerging trends or big ideas in the news. There are also question-and-answer opportunities in which you can connect with experts in your field. That's a great way to connect with others.

Many workers weren't using Zoom, Microsoft Teams, GoToMeeting, or other video conferencing apps before the COVID-19 pandemic, but now these tools have become as routine as texting or using FaceTime on our iPhones. With employees scattered around the country instead of working together in a central office, companies are making very important decisions, including hiring decisions, during virtual meetings. Because of the pandemic, "jumping on Zoom" replaced lunch meetings, boardrooms, and after-hours cocktails. According to CNBC, "In the early days of the pandemic, Zoom's daily meeting participants grew 30 times—from 10 million participants to more than 300 million. In addition, annualized Zoom meeting minutes went from 100 billion in January 2020 to 3 trillion by October. The company also doubled its employee base to 5,000."[6]

I'm here to tell you that Zoom and other video conferencing apps like it aren't going anywhere anytime soon. It's the way we're going to conduct most of our business, including job interviews, from now on. Workers are reluctant to return to the office, and there honestly isn't a good reason for them to be there in industries in which almost everything can be done virtually. If anything, companies realized during the pandemic that many of their employees are more productive working virtually because they can eliminate commuting time and travel to meetings with customers. Instead of spending half the day in the car, employees can stack virtual sales meetings on top of each other.

Zoom also transformed the way we network and connect with coworkers and potential employers. People were more willing to connect or reconnect because it's much easier to jump on Zoom than to jump in an Uber or drive to a restaurant to meet someone for lunch. Plus, people were starving for human interaction while they were isolated during the pandemic. They wanted to see other people's faces and hear their voices—instead of only their spouse's or children's.

Now that virtual networking has been more widely accepted in the professional world, it's easier to reach out to a potential employer or mentor in a faraway state or country. It's as simple as just jumping on Zoom for a few minutes. Most business decisions are going to be made in face-to-face settings, at least the very important ones, so building relationships and establishing a network of trusted colleagues, mentors, and potential employees is essential in developing your career, regardless of how much time you might spend online.

CHAPTER 6

PRINCIPLE 5:
Choose a Team with the Right Talent and Skill Set

*Talent wins games, but teamwork
and intelligence win championships.*
—Michael Jordan

THERE'S AN OLD SAYING about the automobile industry: "Never buy a car that was made on Monday morning." This idea isn't based on hard evidence. It's simply an insinuation that cars assembled at the beginning of the workweek just might be the product of a crew who are recovering from a long weekend of drinking and partying. I don't like generalizing, and I prefer not to toss people or situations into stereotypical categories. But as an entrepreneur who depends on quality labor—both skilled and unskilled—I can't deny that there might be a kernel of truth in the Monday morning theory. In my position, it's certainly something I have to think about. And if you plan to manage employees, it's something you're going to have to think about as well.

You'll find yourself wondering if the teenagers you hired will come to work every day, especially in the aftermath of a global pandemic, when it seems that no one wants to work. You'll find yourself pondering why the production output is lower on Fridays. You'll find yourself constantly assessing and reassessing whether you have the right staff. At a certain point, you'll even have to face something that no one who takes pride in their own abilities wants to admit: your talent is only as good as the talent demonstrated by members of your team.

This is not a subject for debate. It's a fact. Chief executive officers can't afford to be naive about the employees they hire or the contractors that provide the services they outsource. These individuals and entities are key to a successful operation. They are not only responsible for production but are often the first or last line of defense between you and your patrons. They are your company's image, attitude, and voice.

In essence, they fall into three categories: Finders, Minders, and Grinders.

1. **Finders:** A Finder is someone charged with business development. This is the person who is actively identifying prospective new deals, whether it's at the local chamber of commerce, the Black chamber of commerce, country and golf clubs, alumni associations, and anywhere potential

dealmakers—and deals—might be present. The Finder schedules meetings and goes out every night hunting for deals. Ideally, once a Finder identifies a deal, they have a team in place that can turn it over to a Minder.

2. **Minders:** Those in C-suite roles, management, or operations are the Minders: CEO, CFO, CMO, CTO, the chief talent acquisition person, and others, many of whom have MBAs or legal degrees. The Minders collaborate to evaluate and manage a newly identified opportunity and determine whether it should evolve into a business deal.

3. **Grinders:** Grinders are manufacturing or support staff who are tasked, ideally, with working together in a positive environment to produce products and services. They're the guys and gals on the assembly lines, in warehouses filling orders, or the young people at the front counter and in the kitchen of your restaurant.

The success of any business depends on these three interconnected roles. If they aren't filled properly, you can forget about your impeccable credentials or impressive work ethic. No matter how accomplished you are or how good you might be at your craft, it's the people who work for you and with you who will have lasting impacts. There is one exception, however. It's a typical phenomenon that occurs during those lean start-up years when the founder and CEO of the establishment has the honor of wearing all three hats. At the infancy stage of your enterprise, you're the taskmaster. You get to do it all.

If that sounds daunting, don't worry. You won't be the first to fly solo. When Dan Price launched Gravity Payments, a credit card processing service, he was a nineteen-year-old college student working alone in his dorm room. Another young man, Todd Pedersen—best known for Vivent, a home automation service provider—once had the lonely task of running a door-to-door pest control company from a tiny trailer. And during the early 1960s, it wasn't unusual for a certain starry-eyed young songwriter to be up all night, juggling responsibilities for his fledgling recording business. His name was Berry Gordy, and the company was Motown Records.

Driven by passion and pride, Gordy had borrowed close to $1,000 from his family loan fund and set out to leave his thumbprint on the world of music. He was the Finder who scouted the talent and sought funding. He was the Minder who signed the talent, cut the deals, and established a business plan. He was the Grinder who wrote new material for his teenage artists and shaped their careers—all on the first floor of his home on Detroit's West Grand Boulevard.

No matter what age you are, you probably know the rest of this story by heart. Gordy's brainchild exploded into a label recognized all over the world. But along with his success came the growing pains of entrusting his dream to that sea of friends, acquaintances, and strangers called the workforce. They are the talent you and I will eventually need to ensure that our businesses survive and thrive. The catch-22 is that their behavior can build the company's reputation up—or tear it down.

FIVE RULES FOR
MAKING GOOD HIRES

Luckily, there are clever ways to deal with this conundrum. Very early in the game, you have to learn how to identify business talent the way Gordy could identify future stars. Sometimes making the right selection will be obvious. You conduct a probing interview, double-check references, and notice the way the prospective employee is dressed. But your personal impressions, though important, are not foolproof. Over the years, I have developed my own talent acquisition philosophy based on five solid rules.

Hiring Rule #1: The Jockey's Your Best Bet

When it comes to identifying talent that I want to partner with or invest in, I don't bet on the horse. I bet on the jockey. The jockey is the one who makes a business endeavor work. I have questions such as, How hungry is the jockey? How bad does the jockey want it? Is the jockey prepared to grind 24/7 and put all his or her worldly possessions into the deal? To me, the jockey is the most challenging component of business success. Temperament and resilience are critical parts of a jockey's character composite as well, because I've found that most people can't handle failure, nor can they handle success. That's why the vast majority of people who win state lotteries in the United States are broke within a few years.

Hiring Rule #2: Check Out the IQ and the EQ

I hire for brains, and then I try to motivate. I also consciously look for people who are smarter than I am. In defining "smart," academic degrees are often helpful—but not always. Things such as common sense and emotional quotient (EQ) are also important parts of an individual's intellectual makeup. Regarding that hunger I spoke of earlier, I've observed over the years that jockeys who are second-, third-, and fourth-generation college graduates are often not as hungry as individuals who are the first in their families to graduate from college. They typically grew up in more-affluent homes and might not have the same grit and determination to make their own way. I'm not saying it's that way with everybody, but more times than not, the first-generation college students have more fight in them to get what they believe they deserve.

Hiring Rule #3: Know a Person's "Flavor Straw"

I study people and figure out what makes them tick. I observe what makes them laugh and what makes them mad. I notice the way they dress and the kinds of things they talk about. This helps me understand them and influence them.

For instance, people who know me are aware that I'll happily get up and go to the library, but it might take some coaxing to get me to go to the gym. Reading is the "flavor" I enjoy sipping through my straw. Noted psychologist Abraham Maslow, best known for his Hierarchy of Needs theory, said you motivate people by determining what keeps them going beyond six or twelve months.[1] Inspire your employees by learning their "flavor straw." Is it money, recognition, or being with the "in" crowd? Whatever it is, assist them in their quest to find it. If someone likes Diet Pepsi, you wouldn't bring that person ginger ale. In my case, send me knowledge through articles and books.

Warning: When you analyze people, use the information you have gleaned to influence them positively. Never use it as a tool for manipulation.

Hiring Rule #4: Give and Take

Anyone who has children knows that some kids behave better when you promise them a reward, such as a new toy or an outing. But others couldn't care less. You can promise them the moon, yet their grades and attitude won't budge. In a case like that, you might try taking something away. Telling them they can't play their favorite video game or watch a movie will have much more impact than giving them a gift. The same thing applies to the workforce. Some employees are out for the bonuses, the convenient parking space, and being named Office Worker of the Month. Others, though, will work harder just to avoid penalties and hold on to their job. Don't be too negative, however, and remember that positive reinforcement and incentives to do well are what motivate employees more than anything else.

Hiring Rule #5: Encouragement

There are many languages in the world, but one that is universal is a plain, old-fashioned smile. A smile can transform someone's day—including your own. We all have different methods of encouraging one another, but I've been told that my approach is unique. I like walking up to young people and stating point blank, "I have a deal for you. I'll give you ten dollars if you can answer a question." Then I bombard them with various questions about history or everyday life until I find one they can answer. Money is not the important thing here. This is just my way of saying, "Hey, bro, it's going to be alright. You have to stay in the game!"

Of course, this is my own homespun philosophy. I didn't find it in a book, but I did come up with it after a few good and not-so-good experiences forced me to reflect on the example set by my numbers-running Uncle Paul. Yes, I'm talking about him again. He was a character, this is true. But his old-school wit is the slide rule I use when I need to boost employee morale. Uncle Paul never attended business school, but he had a good feel for what worked and what didn't. One of his chief skills was how to interact with people and how to make them feel like a valuable part of the process. Oh, and he never forgot about that "flavor straw." When he made his rounds to pick up the numbers, his conversations usually went something like this:

"Good morning, Miss Wilson. How are you doing? Did you see what happened yesterday on *Search for Tomorrow*? Can you believe that? By the way, that will be $2.20. Miss Wilson, how's your granddaughter? She doing alright? OK, see you tomorrow."

Don't think for a minute that Uncle Paul liked soap operas. Of course he didn't. But Uncle Paul knew how to relate to people. He knew he could connect with them by dangling their favorite carrot. As a result, his customers, and the people he hired, tended to have his back. Meanwhile, they were certain that he had theirs. It doesn't get any easier than that. Today in the global market of conglomerates and multifaceted corporations, the same approach is being utilized, just in different ways. Uncle Paul's habit of catering to the interests of his base is no different than a sales manager lavishing praise on the highest-grossing members of his sales team. It just makes good business sense to treat people well if you expect them to do a good job.

TREAT YOUR PEOPLE WELL

Now, let's take this a step further. Treating people well extends beyond perks like company cars and trips to The Bahamas. It's as plain and simple as the floor beneath your feet. I mean that literally. Just look around at various office spaces and you'll see that contemporary entrepreneurs are going out of their way to include creature comforts that make the job site so appealing that some workers don't want to go home. I'm not suggesting you install colorful, winding playground slides and some of the other trappings you hear about in Silicon Valley. But I am saying it's not a bad idea to create an atmosphere that your employees find enticing. A firm's specific work environment must represent its corporate culture, but that doesn't mean the environment has to be boring.

Take Vitec Automotive, my favorite among the many companies I have launched. Vitec, which I had the pleasure of selling in 2015, had a gym on the premises. My partners and I had it installed because the plant operated twenty-four hours a day, seven days a week. Another hallmark of Vitec was that our employee cubicles had an open-air, bullpen-style layout—similar to that found at Bloomberg L. P., which Michael Bloomberg also employed in New York's city hall during the time he was mayor.

Vitec's C-suite offices were located all the way at the end of the office floor. This meant I had to walk through the cubicles to get to my office, which gave me an opportunity to fraternize with my employees about both personal and business matters. It removed bureaucratic layers and barriers and enabled my employees and I to form deeper connections. I'm a people person, so this allowed me to exercise one of my strengths. In some ways, I might have been more thrilled about the layout than my employees. After all, it was a far cry from the way I had started out. For decades, there were no office spaces at McDonald's, and I had to store the company check ledgers in the trunk of my car. That was my office. When McDonald's finally began to create real offices inside the franchises, it placed them in the basement. Who gets excited about going to a basement office?

With this in mind, I set out to blend the corporate culture of my flagship enterprise, Vitec, into a new facility. A great deal of planning and thought went into everything, from every office's physical layout to how talent was acquired and developed. But at the automotive assembly plant we operate in Alabama, my partners and I had to consider different factors, such as practical logistics. There are no gas stations, diners, or convenience stores selling cigarettes or alcohol for miles outside of the plant. This was deliberately planned to encourage focus and maximum productivity among employees. It prevents employees from taking long lunch breaks, sometimes drinking cans of beer, and then returning to the plant impaired and suboptimal.

There's a big difference between an aesthetically pleasing work environment and an environment filled with distractions that are not conducive to productivity. If you recall my earlier reference to Monday morning cars, you'll understand this decision and others. It could be a thumbs-up on ping-pong tables, which have become clichéd shorthand for the more relaxed nature of tech start-up life. Or it could be like our plant in Alabama, a highly controlled environment where everything the employees need during the workday is found on-site. Companies must create the kind of office and campus setting that aligns with their corporate values.

Back in the 1980s, when Jheri curls and large door knocker earrings were popular, my McDonald's franchise partners and I had a strict policy forbidding those styles. Our employees were told up front that the styles were against the rules and not part of the image we wanted to project. Whenever an employee would pipe up and say, "That's illegal," I'd reply, "you let me worry about that." You have to set the tone at the top, and that's exactly what we did. Every morning, we held leadership meetings that were productive, professional, and tightly run. As leaders, we knew we had to understand our own strengths and weaknesses and build in habits and practices that aligned with our natural rhythms. We also knew we had to understand the strengths and weaknesses of our employees in order to encourage them to use their full potential.

It wasn't easy, but, as Nelson Mandela once said, "It always seems impossible until it is done."[2] I always knew it could be done; I'm a firm believer that you have to *give* more in order to *get* the maximum. So I invest in my staff as well as my businesses. I used to reward my most trusted long-term managers by assigning them the task of getting my next company up and running—and giving them a combination of a salary and a 5 percent equity stake consisting of phantom stock as compensation. (Unlike traditional stock, those who have phantom stock are not eligible to vote at shareholder meetings.)

Once the new company was up and running and had achieved some milestones and profitability, I would give that manager real stock, where they were allowed to vote. As the company grew, I would reward them with additional real stock. When I was ready to launch my next company, we would start the process all over again. I'm known for being generous—some would say to a fault. When I sold Vitec, I gave my employees more money than was required. But it never troubled me because I am blessed, and I wanted to bless my employees as well.

DEALING WITH EMPLOYEE PROBLEMS

On the flip side, every CEO has experienced employee malfeasance, and I'm no exception. Two major incidents come to mind. At Vitec, I experienced corporate fraud by an extremely intelligent young man who had passed the CPA exam at age twenty-one. He was a member of the same fraternal order that I belonged to and was recommended by an employee I trusted. That trust and high-level recommendation gave him access to a major role within Vitec. If it were not for the referral, possibly, I would have followed my gut. Something told me not to hire him because he was too flashy for my taste, and flashy is an odd trait for a finance guy. When my worst fears came to pass—the guy stole from us—I didn't beat myself up. I simply reminded myself that Michael Jordan used to practice free throws while blindfolded. He was honing his skills, perfecting his judgment, and tuning in to the precise maneuver. That's something all of us have to do. It's a nonstop learning process.

Years ago, a CEO who was my star employee left one of my companies, and my partners and I had to avert another near disaster caused by his replacement. The initial mold that creates an automotive part we produce is expensive to build. We discovered that the new CEO we hired was having low-quality molds produced by one of his friends in Wisconsin—and he was pocketing the difference. After this unethical CEO died, we had a $100,000 company life insurance policy on him, but his family had no personal insurance policy. His wife ended up in great financial distress. His widow phoned me about her situation, and I met with her and listened to what she had to say.

Ultimately, I gave her half the $100,000 policy.

News that I had chosen to take the honorable route to help the widow of a man who was less than honorable to our company rapidly spread throughout the supplier community. I didn't concern myself with who *he* was because I know who *I* am—and I knew I would continue to be blessed and get that money back in multiples.

IDENTIFYING GOOD FITS AND BAD FITS

My master's degree is in social work, and I remain a social worker at heart. I know that when it comes to an individual's character, ethics and integrity are the bedrock. This has always been an integral part of my hiring philosophy and the basis for the way I relate to employees, including managers. This means I am deft in analyzing people, and I cue in on what makes sense and those things in someone's profile that are at odds or amiss. I also stay on the lookout for what's known as "good fits" and "bad fits." I've seen bad fits undermine the careers of some very talented individuals.

Once I hired a CFO who had earned an undergraduate degree from the University of Maryland and an MBA from Harvard University—the perfect background for our company. Or so I thought. This guy showed up at work one day wearing a black shoe on one foot and a brown shoe on the other. His odd habits didn't end with his personal appearance.

When you were unfortunate enough to ride in his car, you felt like you were sitting in the junk-hauling truck from the 1970s sitcom *Sanford and Son*. He had a first-rate mind, but his lack of social skills held him back from working in places like Wall Street. Eventually, he wound up in China working for a major national company. I shudder at the fact that there are so many who lose out on opportunities and promotions because they cannot make the cultural and social leap needed to be a "good fit."

A "good fit" means the individual is a team player who has the appropriate mindset and a clear understanding of the corporate culture. These are essential traits for employees. When it comes to a business partner, these traits are so important that they're nonnegotiable. If you decide to partner with someone, make sure the two of you have shared values that can translate into a harmonious working relationship. Ask yourself:

Do they have good rapport with you and the rest of the management team?

Can they handle stress?

Are they insubordinate?

Can they go with the flow?

Are they trustworthy?

Do they have a history of loyalty?

Keep in mind that a business partnership is like a marriage. It can bring out the best or the worst in you. Compatible partners push each other's talents to the surface by playing off each other's strengths. Magic Johnson was a better basketball player when he played against Larry Bird, and Bird was better when he played against Magic. When a sharp knife meets a sharp knife, both knives become sharper—or, as the Bible puts it, "iron sharpens iron." Some individuals are born salespeople, but a born salesperson without some training and feedback from management and colleagues can be a loose cannon. Likewise, some people are just natural talent-finders and, by employing their interpersonal skills, are able to seek out the best in people. They, too, need formal training and feedback to refine their skills.

In an ideal business relationship, the company flourishes. In a bad one, tempers flare, money is lost, and businesses are liquidated. In 2001, the Los Angeles Lakers built one of the NBA's first "dream teams" by adding All-Stars Steve Nash and Dwight Howard to a lineup that already included Kobe Bryant, Paul Gasol, and Metta World Peace. With a lineup of five of the game's best players, the Lakers were supposed to contend for a world championship. Instead, their coach was fired after only five games, the Lakers struggled to make the playoffs, and they were eliminated in the first round. There were too many egos—and just one basketball—and they couldn't get along.

WHEN TO PARTNER—OR NOT

The goal of a good partnership is mutual respect and understanding. And to achieve that, you will have to operate within certain parameters that everyone has agreed are in the best interests of the company. If that's not the case, do not enter into a partnership. Period. Clearly, they are not for everyone.

Before jumping into a partnership, you should ask yourself if you really need it and, if so, why. I have found that there are three legitimate reasons for a partnership:

1. You need more money.

2. You have the money, but you need a complementary partner who fills in the talent gap.

3. You need political expediency.

If you don't fall into any of these categories, a partnership might not be for you. But if you determine that a partnership is your cup of tea, make certain you actually know this person and know him or her *well*. Make sure this person is someone who can efficiently execute plans and handle being in the midst of a storm. Just as importantly, ensure that you are going by what you have experienced (as in working with this person in the past) and not what you have heard. After you have dotted your i's and crossed all your t's, you'll be ready to offer Joe Blow an equity stake in your firm.

GROWING WITH A PARTNER

Sylvester Hester, my business partner of nearly thirty years, has started several companies for me, employing the method I mentioned earlier. I would give him 5 percent phantom stock. The business would grow. He would hit some home runs. I would then give him "real," or voting, stock. He would hit some more home runs. I would give him more real stock, then he would move on to our next start-up business and do the same. Sylvester is trustworthy and, as a result, we have a great relationship. He joined my company Regal Plastics in 1987 after being the first Black student to graduate from Ferris State University with a degree in plastics engineering. We soon discovered that he had a natural ability to sell. This filled a major talent gap. Between 1991 and 1996, Regal went from a company with $13 million in sales to $33 million in sales.

As Sylvester likes to tell it, this occurred at a time when globalization was affecting the interaction between automotive companies and suppliers. Under this new model, automotive suppliers were not paid until the end of the year. Everything was about cost containment. Tier-one suppliers became tier-two suppliers to larger companies. As this new trend progressed, tier-one companies began to outsource their noncore businesses and most aspects of the core business were brought in-house. Meanwhile, the auto business was moving to the South. In 1998, Sylvester relocated to Atlanta and started one of my new companies, ARD Logistics. Johnson Controls was the first tier-one company to outsource its logistics to us. This was a major home run. In 2001, Sylvester hit another home run with a contract for our plant in Alabama and again in 2003 with the opening of the ARD office in Charleston, South Carolina.

With each success, he received a larger share of the companies he started. ARD Logistics continues to diversify into food and beverage, aerospace, and the government sector. Over the past thirty years, Sylvester has worked to earn his new title of president and CEO of Global Alliance, the umbrella company for most of my automotive companies.

However, I'm at a point in my life—and our partnership—where I'm not open to taking on more risk. In order to expand your business, a bank will want you to back a loan with a personal guarantee. This means if the loan goes under, you will be expected to write the check to cover it. To minimize the potential of such a problem, I created a special arrangement with Sylvester and the bank. Under this arrangement, he is taking the business in a direction of growth, and he and I are handling the necessary guarantees in a more equitable manner. As a result, Sylvester will become the primary manager and owner at a future date.

If I'm a majority owner in a business, I try to be hands-on. I have to be personally involved and vested. I'm not going to be in Florida and have my partner managing a company in Oklahoma with my million dollars on the line, even though we've known each other so long he can practically count my money. Trust is not the issue here; it is my lack of appetite for extra risks. As has happened with my relationship with my business partner, who is decades younger than I am, there's a point when the difference in age and number of years each partner has been in business can come into play. I don't need additional growth to maintain my current lifestyle. Revenue from my current portfolio of companies amply covers all my business and personal needs.

EXITING A PARTNERSHIP

Any partnerships I still maintain are a matter of choice. Just as I knew how to get into them, I also know how to get out.

This is a basic business skill: you have to know when to hold them and when to fold them. Part of creating a business is also developing an exit strategy where you and any partners agree on one or more desired future outcomes for the business, such as a merger, an initial public offering (IPO), or a sale. One of the ways to benefit from a business is to build it and sell it. The latter is known as *harvesting*. In a partnership, this can become problematic. What do you do if you want to harvest the business in your exit strategy and your partner isn't ready to harvest? This is common, especially among partners at different ages or life cycles. To avoid clashing, a company must take two critical steps in advance:

Have a Buy/Sell Agreement in Place: This agreement should establish that, one day, one of the partners is going to exit the business. The company should be prepared for this financially and operationally.

Be Prepared for a Partner's Untimely Death: The family of a deceased partner may know that, prior to death, the partner had a $3 million equity stake in the company. That might be true, but that doesn't necessarily mean that the company has $3 million in liquid assets to compensate the spouse of the deceased for that ownership stake. Companies typically fund them via insurance policies. This measure should be addressed in the buy/sell agreement.

Without these agreements, handling or dissolving a partnership can be as challenging as the rockiest marriage or the most bitter divorce. Yet I must admit, in a good union, the benefits far outweigh the problems.

INSIDE PARTNERS
AND OUTSIDE PARTNERS

Partnerships allow those involved to divide and multiply. One partner is charged primarily with internal matters related to the company's business (Mr. or Mrs. Inside), while the other focuses on external matters (Mr. or Mrs. Outside). One of you is taking care of operations and personnel while the other is focused on finance and sales. One is hunting and the other is skinning. The roles are distinct but complementary.

You even see this in the typical university environment, which has a provost who deals with the professors and a president who goes out and raises money. It's an inside-outside division of labor. One person has his hands in and the other has his hands out. Why is that so important? I can answer that with a story that would raise the eyebrows of any savvy entrepreneur. One of my young mentees wanted to open a Burger King or McDonald's franchise with his two brothers. Their father had died a few years earlier and, collectively, they had $400,000 in seed capital. They lived in Flint, Michigan, but made frequent visits to Lansing, Michigan. From my mentee's perspective, Lansing was an excellent franchise site because he and his brothers had enough revenue to hire someone to relocate to the city and operate the restaurant for them.

I took a deep breath, then asked, "Where's your wife?"

He replied, "She's here in the house."

I said, "Put her on the phone. I want to talk to her."

He wasn't sure what to say. After a brief pause, he

responded, "Why do you want to speak with my wife?"

I replied, "I want to tell her she married a d--- fool! Think about what you just told me. You're going to take $400,000 of your family's money and hire somebody to go to Lansing and operate your business while you go to work somewhere else and in some other city every day. What makes you think that's going to work?"

"People do it every day," he answered.

"Trust me," I said. "I've been in this business almost fifty years. If I ran your restaurant, and I ran it very well, I would suck up the little bit of profit you make—and you wouldn't notice it. I would 'fee' you to death. I would have management fees, and I would have my cousin on the payroll."

He didn't get it, but one of his brothers did. That sibling called back and said, "My brother told me what you said to him. Thank you very much."

Be very clear if you're starting a business: you have to manage *your own* business. In my line of work, I'm frugal and practical. I'm not going to invest in anything I'm not a part of operationally. There may come a time when you can hire and begin to outsource some of the tasks, but by that time you will know every pore, fiber, and tick of your business. Outsourcing makes sense only if you're making enough to absorb the management fees and still turn a healthy profit.

I could have taken a more step-by-step approach by talking to my mentee about the dangers of absentee management, but I went for the jugular and basically told him, "You're crazy! I own five McDonald's and five other businesses around the country, and I can guarantee you that, at this very moment, there is someone in one of my businesses acting like an owner and taking profits, or materials, or French fries, or drinks that they do not own. And they're giving it away." That's what corporate jargon refers to as *shrinkage*.

One of my young employees casually told me a story about how she had run out of money and her girlfriend who worked at a sandwich shop gave her something to eat for free. This was an example of an employee generously gifting something that he or she does not own. Another young McDonald's employee at my Grosse Pointe, Michigan, location gave away a free soda to a visiting friend while I was there. When I pointed out what she had done, she said, "Dr. Pickard, that's my friend. I just gave him a Coke." Because that was her friend, she felt it was not stealing. I kindly, but firmly, let her know that it was.

This brings me back to my original point. Your business is in the hands of your Finders, Minders, and Grinders. Choose them wisely and treat them with respect, but give them only as much rope as they need. You are the eyes, ears, and brains behind your establishment. You're the person steering the ship and shepherding the crew. That might mean a whole lot of hours and more sacrifices than you anticipated. But there are only three ways for those with talent and ambition to get to their destination: crawl, walk, and then run.

* * *

Surviving the Shift

In 1908, Norway's Roald Amundsen was preparing for a dangerous mission to become the first man to reach the North Pole. He was awarded money by the Norwegian Parliament to fund the polar expedition. He borrowed a four-hundred-ton schooner and recruited a crew of brave men to join him on the sail through the icy Bering Strait.

Then, just before Amundsen and his men were to set sail, he learned that the American explorer Robert E. Peary had reached the North Pole in April 1909. Undeterred, Amundsen continued to get ready and told no one but his brother that they were going somewhere else instead. He didn't want the crew to find out someone had already stolen their glory. When the Norwegian was met with the devastating news that someone had already reached the North Pole, he turned his ship around and became the first explorer to reach the *South* Pole on December 14, 1911.

How many times will you have to change your plans or the direction of your company as an entrepreneur? What will you do when whitecaps are crashing into your business from all sides? Changing course is never easy, especially in the middle of a worldwide pandemic. Entrepreneurs have to be quick on their feet—calm, cool, and collected—and willing to twist and turn all while keeping the big picture in focus.

The COVID-19 pandemic forced business leaders and companies to reexamine what really mattered to their employees and consumers. They've had to be more flexible and empathetic about salary, benefits, career development, and working conditions. The pandemic emboldened the American worker, and the era of nine-to-five days and forty-hour weeks in cramped office cubicles seems to be over. Employees want better pay, increased benefits, shorter workweeks, and the ability to work from home.

As an entrepreneur, you were already going to have to wear many hats. Now you're going to have to wear even more while still trying to focus on the bottom line—making your business as profitable as possible. How will you do that? In addition to the skills we discussed above, you'll need five must-have abilities to survive post-pandemic.

PIVOTING QUICKLY

When the COVID-19 pandemic hit, governors in states across the country shuttered bars, restaurants, gyms, and other high-traffic businesses to keep the virus from spreading. Restaurant sales took a huge hit for a couple of months, but as people ran out of groceries, grew tired of cooking at home, or just wanted to get out of the house, drive-thru lanes became more popular than ever before.

With dining rooms closed, restaurant owners like myself had to devote most of their time to figuring out how to make their drive-thru lanes as efficient and profitable as possible. We had to pivot quickly, kind of like LeBron James in the lane, to make things work. And guess what? Sales at my McDonald's franchises soared through the roof, and I wasn't alone. According to marketing research company NPD Group, drive-thru lanes accounted for 44 percent of off-premises orders across the entire restaurant industry in 2020.[3] Many restaurants not only survived—they thrived.

Drive-thru lanes have become so profitable that many restaurant chains are expanding them. Some restaurants are even eliminating dining rooms, which cuts some overhead costs, reduces the number of employees you need, and turns over customers more quickly. Restaurants that didn't have drive-thru lanes in the past, such as Shake Shack and Chipotle, are now adding them. Remember that change is inevitable—except from a vending machine! As Sam Cooke so beautifully sang in "A Change Is Gonna Come," "It's been a long, a long time comin'. But I know, a change gonna come. Oh yes, it will."

CRISIS MANAGEMENT

Business leaders around the world are used to dealing with crises, but few of them have ever been blindsided by something as big and devastating as the COVID-19 pandemic. It was like being hit with a Mike Tyson uppercut when you weren't looking! Crisis is when a leader's true colors are revealed, and how they respond during a time of fear, dread, and uncertainty will ultimately determine whether their company will survive. As the author John C. Maxwell wrote, "A leader is one who knows the way, goes the way, and shows the way."[4] It's a privilege to lead, and you have to take care of the little things each day to ensure that you're ready when something big slaps you in the face.

The job-search site Glassdoor conducted a survey of the highest-rated CEOs during the pandemic based on feedback from their employees. It's not surprising that there were common threads among those who were given the highest marks: "prioritizing work-life balance, taking care of employees' overall well-being, offering flexible and/or remote working policies, establishing strong health benefits and maintaining frequent, clear communication."[5] When the going got tough, those leaders stepped up, made difficult decisions, communicated clearly, and found the right balance between doing what was best for their employees and what was best for their companies. Follow their examples.

PATIENCE

Being an entrepreneur already required a boatload of patience. As the boss, it's your job to deal with customers and employees, and sometimes that isn't easy. Remember that customers are like teeth: ignore them, and they will go away. And, because of the pandemic, the same is now true of your employees.

For whatever reason, many young people walked away from their jobs during the pandemic and never went back. As *TIME* noted in October 2021,

This is the highest mass resignation the U.S. has seen since 2019, pre-pandemic, and the numbers are still rising. In June, 3.9 million quit. In July, it was another 3.9 million. In August, 4.3 million. The numbers are even more notable for young workers:

in September, nearly a quarter of workers ages 20 to 34 were not considered part of the U.S. workforce—some 14 million Americans, according to the Bureau of Labor Statistics, who were neither working nor looking for work.[6]

Economists are calling it the "Great Resignation." In October 2021, there were 10.4 million jobs in the United States that were unfilled, according to *TIME*.[7] Drive up and down any commercial area in any American city or town, and odds are you'll see plenty of Help Wanted signs. With so many unfilled jobs, workers have leverage, and business owners will have to find the right balance between what's *fair* and what's *sustainable* long-term for their companies. It won't be easy.

I know the owner of a handful of fast-food franchises of a popular national chain in the Nashville area. Before the pandemic, he needed about forty-five employees to run each one of his stores. During the summer of 2021, he was down to *three* employees at one of his busiest locations. He and his partner were in the kitchen cooking food and serving customers. That's not what they signed up for when they shelled out a couple million dollars to open the franchises. But they're doing what they have to do to keep the doors open. That's what leaders do. They're now more patient with their employees because it's not easy to find a replacement if one quits.

"If someone doesn't show up for work, we'll call them and say, 'Hey, you coming in tomorrow?'" he said. "In the past, we would have fired them on the spot."

That's the new reality facing entrepreneurs. Remember

what the author Joyce Meyer said: "Patience is not the ability to wait, but the ability to keep a good attitude while waiting."[8] Keep a smile on your face, listen to your employees' concerns and wants, and then decide what is fair.

Develop Others

As noted, retaining your employees, especially the good ones, is one of the keys to running a successful business, and that's never been more difficult to do. It costs time and money to hire new employees, and the worst thing you can do is have a revolving door in your HR department. In the past, you could retain your best employees by paying above-average salaries, offering competitive benefits, and giving them a fun and comfortable place to work. That's not enough anymore.

Now employees want the comfort of knowing there's a vertical trajectory where they're working. If you hire a guy to be a car salesman, he might want assurances that he'll be considered for an assistant manager's position within a year. Then he'll want to be in charge of used cars, the repair shop, and eventually become general manager. Heck, a lot of the Gen Zers and millennials don't even want to start on the ground floor anymore.

More and more companies are offering extraordinary perks such as reimbursed tuition or even free college without out-of-pocket costs for their employees. National brands such as Walmart, Target, Hormel Foods, Chick-fil-A, Chase Bank, Publix, and The Home Depot are doing it. Other companies are offering signing bonuses and higher pay than they normally would. The market for employees is that competitive.

The best thing you can do is treat your employees like family. Take care of them, listen to them, and treat them as you would want to be treated. If you're not in a position to offer tuition, find other ways to provide learning opportunities to your employees. Quiz them about what they like and dislike about their job. Ask them what parts are rewarding and challenging. Ask them about their short- and long-term goals. Make them feel like there's a future within your business, even if they're an employee who just started in an entry-level position. Remember what I said: you're only as good as your Finders, Minders, and Grinders.

RESILIENCY

Every entrepreneur is going to get knocked down; it's inevitable. When the pandemic hit, Stephen Natoli, owner of Natoli's Italian Deli in Secaucus, New Jersey, lost all his catering business, which accounted for about half of his total revenue. When the state shut down inside dining, he moved all the restaurant's seating outside and turned his dining room into a grocery store. It was so successful, he opened another grocery store on the other side of town.

"We picked up about 20 to 25 percent of the business we lost in catering," Natoli told *TIME*. "I decided to keep that 20 to 25 percent and when catering comes back, I want to bang that on top."[9]

About three million businesses closed during the first year of the pandemic. Only the strong ones survived, including the ones that got knocked down, figured it out, and hit the reset button.

The worldwide pandemic proved once again that business owners and leaders must have the ability to pivot quickly, think fast, and make necessary and difficult changes. How will you react when the you-know-what hits the fan? If you've surrounded yourself with the right people—the Finders, Minders, and Grinders I told you about earlier—you'll have a much better chance of surviving.

CHAPTER 7

PRINCIPLE 6:
Do Not Overreact
to Failure

*In every adversity lies the seed
of an equal or greater opportunity.*
—Napoleon Hill

I WAITED. In the summer of 2000, I participated in a one-day entrepreneur conference at Harvard University in Boston. But I had a
special concern, and no one had addressed it. So I kept waiting.
Hundreds of people streamed in and out of the assembly rooms.
Meanwhile, speaker after speaker discussed project management,
joint ventures, employee retention, and spreadsheets.

I continued to wait.

The next talk I attended dealt with global enterprise. As a
business owner with global reach, I found it highly beneficial.
But it wasn't the food my soul craved.

So, I waited some more.

Another hour passed, the convention ended, and I returned home, puzzled. Every presenter had talked about success, but not a single one had touched on that hidden little fear that lurks in the back of all entrepreneurs' minds: *What happens if I fail? What should I do when the doors slam, when the bottom falls out, when all loan applications have been denied?*

Of course, I wasn't exactly a neophyte in this area. Although my McDonald's franchises were thriving and my auto supply businesses were doing well, I had recently come frighteningly close to financial paralysis. I pulled through without a scar. But I'm a realist. I wanted to be equipped in case I find myself in a similar situation in the future. And don't forget, I had been schooled by the best of them, my Uncle Paul. He was a pragmatist who warned me that businesses are always a risk. According to my wise old uncle, anyone who stays in the game long enough will stare rejection, disappointment, and possibly bankruptcy in the face.

That's why I was disappointed in the agenda at that conference. I had hoped to receive a few tips about remaining positive while on the brink of defeat. I was interested in hearing someone explain the cyclical nature of entrepreneurship and tell me how to weather the winds of change if, once again, they should happen to blow my way. What I hadn't anticipated was avoidance and denial. I didn't realize the topic would be swept under the rug.

Fortunately, attitudes have flip-flopped since then. Today failure is being examined, even romanticized. In order to prepare students for the "real" world, failure is an elective course at certain universities and high schools. In fact, the School of the Art Institute of Chicago encourages students to enroll in the class titled "The Ethics and Aesthetics of Failure."

It doesn't stop there. Failure is the subject of newspaper and magazine articles and a popular theme in contemporary motivational lectures. So much ado is being made about it, you might find yourself wondering if it has become vogue. It has not. But what has occurred is an acceptance that things don't always go right, business endeavors included.

These days, there is a tacit realization that failure is something that simply comes with entrepreneurship territory. It's like gravity. Sometimes you fall and, well, falling is natural. All you have to do is get up. When you do, you'll be comforted by the awareness that your situation wasn't so bad after all. In fact, you just joined a pretty impressive club.

Did you know that Oprah Winfrey was fired from one of her first TV news reporter jobs because she wasn't the "right fit"? Then there's our nation's sixteenth president, Abraham Lincoln. Before he made it to the White House, he lost seven elections and struck out in business three times.

Yet they were not deterred. Their names are well known today because they understood one of life's most valuable lessons: if at first you don't succeed, you're about average.

Winfrey and Lincoln knew that failure is not the exception; it is the rule. They didn't allow their careers to be destroyed or their drive to be dampened by that dreaded little life episode that eventually knocks on everyone's door. They realized that failure is as American as apple pie and Chevrolet. It is not a death sentence. It is not the enemy, and it is not the last word. According to the Small Business Administration, around 33 percent of all new ventures with employees close down within two years and about 50 percent are out of business in five years. Only one in four is still around fifteen years after opening.[1] Yet many are successful when they stay the course and dare to cast their net again and again. As novelist F. Scott Fitzgerald once said, "Never confuse a single defeat with a final defeat."[2] Jazz legend Miles Davis said something similar. In his own enigmatic way, Miles remarked, "When you hit a wrong note, it's the next note you play that determines if it's good or bad."[3]

As an entrepreneur, that "next note" is up to you. You can let your mistakes engulf you or you can keep pressing forward. In his effort to create the light bulb, Thomas Edison failed nearly one thousand times. But Edison, who had been told by his teachers that he was "too stupid to learn anything," had developed pretty thick skin by then. He saw all his efforts as a success. He said he had merely discovered a thousand ways *not* to achieve his goal.[4]

Think about the top ten entrepreneurs in the United States. Virtually all of them failed once or twice in a business venture due to lack of knowledge or funding. In some cases, a misstep placed them so far behind the market's conditions that they were forced to leave the race—temporarily. There's a big difference between leaving and quitting. Make no mistake about it: success is the kissing cousin of failure. The people on top are there because they refused to remain on the bottom. Here are a few of these rags-to-riches, failure-before-success stories.

Tyler Perry

From 1992 to 1998, every stage play Perry produced failed. In most cases, he lost all of the money he had invested, and in some instances, not a single person showed up for a performance. Tyler said that each time a production did poorly, he "learned something new." He would apply what he learned to the next show and the next. In 1998, he decided to take a revamped version of his failed play, *I Know I've Been Changed*, on the road. That's when he finally found success. Eventually, Perry went from living in his car to living in a mansion and writing, producing, directing, and/or acting in twenty-eight films and fifteen television shows. He is best known for his *Madea* franchise, which has grossed more than $660 million alone. In 2021, *Forbes* estimated his net worth at $1 billion. Perry says, "What you may perceive as failure may very well be an opportunity to learn, grow, get better, and prepare for the next level."[5]

Walt Disney

A high school dropout, Disney was fired from a Missouri newspaper because his editor said he "lacked imagination." Later he launched a business, Laugh-o-Gram Studios, which went bankrupt. One night, while broke, tired, and still pursuing his dream of animation, he noticed a mouse sitting in the middle of the shabby room he was renting. The mouse stared at Disney and, in a state of frustration, Disney stared back. He imagined the critter was saying, "Man, you're so poor you don't even have any cheese in this place." Disney doodled the mouse, and it became the prototype for one of the biggest icons the cartoon industry has ever known. In the 2020 fiscal year, the Walt Disney Company generated total revenue of $65.4 billion.[6]

Sidney Poitier

At the age of sixteen, Sidney Poitier, a Bahamas native, worked as a delivery boy in a white Miami neighborhood. Unaware of American racial politics in the mid-1940s, he made a package drop-off to the front door instead of the back door. When he returned home that evening, he was told that the Ku Klux Klan was looking for him. Poitier used his meager earnings to buy a one-way bus ticket as far from Florida as he could get. He ended up in New York. After two years of struggle, he spotted an ad for the American Negro Theater and—out of desperation—decided to try out. He failed miserably. His Caribbean accent and poor reading skills made him a laughing-stock during the audition.

Disgraced, Poitier found a night job as a dishwasher and spent his free time perfecting his voice inflections and honing his reading and acting skills. By the time he was twenty-five, Poitier was starring in major motion pictures and on his way to becoming the first Black male to receive an Academy Award for Best Actor. Poitier said, "I always wanted to be someone better the next day than I was the day before."[7]

Reginald Lewis

When he was a student at Virginia State College, Lewis had a big decision to make. Should he own up to a shoulder injury and thereby risk losing his football scholarship and possible National Football League career? Or should he endure the pain and avoid the specter of failure? He accepted failure. Several years later, he was graduating from Harvard Law School and preparing himself for corporate America. But his first attempt to buy a business failed. Two years later, he bid on a company that manufactured lawn chairs. The bid failed. He failed again in a 1983 effort to purchase a radio station group. Lewis armed himself with knowledge by studying the details of public deals, both successful and unsuccessful.

In 1984, Lewis, author of *Why Should White Guys Have All the Fun?*, bought McCall's Patterns, a sewing pattern company. After doubling its earnings, he sold it for more than twice its purchase price. Then he won a bidding war for Beatrice International, a food conglomerate with $2 billion in annual sales, making him the top Black-owned business owner in the nation in 1987. In 1992, *Forbes* included him among the four hundred richest Americans with a net worth of $400 million.[8]

Tom Monaghan

The founder of Domino's Pizza and former owner of the Detroit Tigers was once an example of failure personified. Monaghan grew up in a Catholic orphanage and spent much of his childhood daydreaming about owning a chain of ice cream stands or a fleet of tractors. But his early adult years were fraught with disappointment, and the business world wasn't as welcoming as he had hoped. In one instance, a potential business partner stole close to $2,000—Monaghan's life savings—and left town.

Later Monaghan started a pizza company in Ypsilanti, Michigan, with his brother. However, the two were forced to file for bankruptcy, and at one point the struggling operation burned down. Monaghan's brother eventually gave up on the business and asked Tom to buy him out. All Tom had to offer was the little Volkswagen Beetle he used for pizza delivery. The brother accepted, and Tom moved to Ann Arbor and went solo. It was there, several failures later, that his vision became reality. Today Domino's is the largest pizza franchise in the world with more than $12 billion in annual gross sales and about sixteen thousand stores in eighty-five countries.[9] If you visit the Ann Arbor headquarters, you'll see a shiny, refurbished 1954 Volkswagen in the lobby—a monument to the power of sheer persistence.

Do you see the pattern? Real entrepreneurs don't shrink at the first sign of trouble. Real entrepreneurs buckle up and shift to a higher gear. As an up-and-comer, you must embrace both risk and opportunity, then do your personal due diligence. Decide, in advance, how you would handle it if your venture became sidetracked. Would you be humiliated, or would you be ready to tackle it and bounce back? Reactions are varied because failure has a different impact depending on your background, your expectations, and the number of people bragging about you, rooting for you, or eagerly anticipating your golden victory.

I still remember the time one of the instructors at the community college I once attended announced in class that a certain student had flunked out of school. I really felt for this young lady because, obviously, if you fail community college, that's pretty much rock bottom. I also couldn't help but notice the look of profound sadness on our instructor's face. She explained that the student had to go home and give her parents, her siblings, her church associates, and her friends the news that she had failed.

At the time, I sort of figured the emotional aspect of failure wouldn't be that significant for me. I didn't have to factor in other people's expectations because that really wasn't on my radar screen. No one expected me to succeed. When I shattered those notions and soared to greater heights, it was a pleasant surprise for everyone, including me. This newfound success placed me on a higher pedestal and a totally different trajectory. My world changed and so did my standards, my circle, my peers. People believed in me. Newspapers were writing articles about me. I was raking in awards and flying around the country, hobnobbing with the big wheels. Things that hadn't mattered to me mattered all of a sudden.

With this adjusted perception came the pressure of wanting to make sure I didn't let anyone down. After I had at least eight or nine McDonald's franchises under my belt, I began to explore the horizon for other opportunities. A big one came in the form of Regal Plastics, a bankrupt auto supply business. Why would I buy a company that was in bankruptcy? Well, for one thing, it was cheap. For another, I firmly believed in my abilities. I assumed that the company's problems were the result of poor management.

In order to get the ball rolling, I had to meet with a committee of Regal Plastic's creditors and assure them that I had what it took to turn their lemon into lemonade. At the time, Regal Plastics was one of the few companies that produced shifter knobs for the gear sticks in automatic and stick shift cars for one of the Big Three automakers, and it was critically important to them that the fragile auto supply company survive. During my meeting, I explained how I would breathe new life into this endeavor. I also made a request to the auto supplier that the money they were owed by Regal Plastic be turned into long-term debt. As part of this request, I agreed to pay back forty cents on every dollar.

Fortunately, the credit committee voted unanimously to let me give it a whirl. I was ecstatic. Keep in mind, my McDonald's franchises were doing well. But I was eager to expand. Regal Plastics was my first step outside of the fast-food industry and into a bold new arena.

Within a few years, my team and I had revived the business and were prepared to pay back the creditors eight months before the scheduled payoff date. My advisory committee members were so impressed they tried to convince me that, because I had turned things around in record time, the creditors would accept ten cents on the dollar as a payback. Something about that didn't feel quite right to me. Against their wishes, I stuck with my original commitment and paid back the loan at forty cents on the dollar. Now the company was rocking and rolling, and my income had increased exponentially.

Little did I know, disaster was lurking in the shadows. Ten years down the road, the auto company that did business with Regal Plastics gave us a major order for the interior of a new car they were just beginning to manufacture. To fill this order, we had to go from two plants to six plants. That meant buying more buildings, hiring additional employees, and acquiring new equipment. I saw it as an exciting prospect and a chance for tremendous progress. But my calculations and my confidence were out of sync. Regal Plastics was not ready financially or organizationally for such a huge leap. We didn't have the right people in the right places, and with our new plants and new equipment, we had taken on far too much debt. To make matters worse, the new cars didn't sell. The whole thing was a mess.

In hindsight, we should have said *no* to the expansion. But nobody says no when they think they're good. We were good, but apparently not *that* good. In plain and simple business lexicon, we were "hugging ourselves to death."

This experience, which lasted eight long, nightmarish months, turned out to be the worst of my career. My best right-hand man had already moved on to another opportunity. The car had failed. We had more debt than we could handle, and we couldn't pay our creditors. Operationally, we were failing drastically.

I could say, at this point, that I sucked it up and shrugged, "Hey, stuff happens." Or that I reflected on the infamous words of author Napoleon Hill, who said, "Every adversity, every failure, every heartache, carries with it the seed of an equal or greater benefit."[10] I could even say that I turned to one of Michael Jordan's best-known quotes: "I've missed more than 9,000 shots in my career. I've lost almost three hundred games. Twenty-six times, I've been trusted to take the game winning shot and missed. I've failed over and over again in my life. And that is why I succeed."[11]

Failure is just part of the journey to success. Remember that Jordan, the greatest player of his generation, spent his sophomore year in high school playing on the *junior* varsity team. He never quit and used that slight as motivation throughout his Hall of Fame career. "I can accept failure, everyone fails at something," he once said. "But I can't accept not trying."[12]

Jack Canfield and Mark Victor Hansen, authors of the *Chicken Soup for the Soul* book series, were rejected 144 times by publishers. Today, there are 250 titles in this memorable series that have been published in one hundred countries and in forty-three languages. By 2013, more than 500 million of the books had been sold worldwide—or about 3.4 million for every rejection they received. "If we had given up after one hundred publishers, I likely would not be where I am now," Canfield said. "I encourage you to reject rejection. If someone says no, just say, NEXT!"[13]

It might surprise you that the most successful hitters in Major League Baseball history, the Hall of Famers such as Tony Gwynn,

Ted Williams, Pete Rose, and Henry Aaron, failed in about seven of every ten at-bats. That's right, simply having a .300 average will earn you hundreds of millions in America's pastime. It's not easy hitting 100-mph fastballs and sweeping curves. Babe Ruth, who was the home run king until Aaron came along, once said, "Every strike brings me closer to the next home run."[14]

Yes, I could say that I clung to these pearls of wisdom, but I'd be lying. For the first time on my entrepreneurial path, failure was looming before me like a dark tornado, and it depressed me in ways I can barely explain. When you're grappling with a business fiasco, it's as harrowing as a personal crisis, but in many ways it can be worse. The public nature of your problem—litigation, court orders, and pressure from suppliers, employees, accountants, lawyers, and your banker—can make it heavier. And it can cause you to withdraw. I was losing weight as well as sleep. I had no desire to go to social functions because I thought everyone knew about my ordeal.

Friends told me that every company had problems and that I shouldn't let my business woes stop me from getting out and having fun. Still, I refused. All my attention was focused on an upcoming meeting that had been arranged between me and the credit committee.

I'll never forget that day. I had to drive to a hotel at Detroit Metropolitan Airport to stand in front of a group of irate creditors and try to explain what went wrong. I was so nervous, my palms were sweating and my heart was racing. I had never failed in business before, and here I was at this very public event, hanging on by my fingernails.

As I approached the podium and looked into those angry eyes, I recognized many were the same individuals I had stood before ten years earlier to make my initial pitch. Most were there—the people who supplied the cardboard boxes, the sales reps, the vendors who provided tools. Only one original creditor was missing—his position was now being handled by his son. In all, there were about one hundred men and women pointing, hollering, and cursing at me.

I cleared my throat and spoke: "You're looking at the guy who made the decision to take on all of this business," I said. "And it was more than we could chew."

The shouting escalated. But before I could utter another word, a guy stood up and asked everyone to calm down. He reminded the group that I had run a successful business for ten years and had paid them all back forty cents on the dollar in a timely manner.

"Everyone in this room got their check, and no one sent the check back," he said. "So we have made money with him. He has grown the business, tripled it in size, and he admitted he overexpanded."

He continued: "Once you finish screaming and yelling, you need to think about something. If you force him into bankruptcy, we get pennies. He's paid the money back before. That's critical. He'll pay it back again."

After another couple of weeks and a second meeting, I was granted additional time to work out Regal Plastics's problems. Within six months, I was able to orchestrate an orderly wind-down of the company so I could eventually exit it completely.

In the meantime, I began to recall my late Uncle Paul's guidance, as always, and reminded myself that failing is an intrinsic aspect of success and as much a part of being in business as securing a loan or writing a check. Often, it's a step in the right direction.

I also learned that failure is not the challenge. The challenge is what you do with the failure. In *Think and Grow Rich*, Napoleon Hill wrote,

> *Before success comes in any man's life, he is sure to meet with much temporary defeat and, perhaps, some failure. When defeat overtakes a man, the easiest and most logical thing to do is to quit. That is exactly what the majority of men do. More than 500 of the most successful men this country has ever known told the author their greatest success came just one step beyond the point at which defeat had overtaken them.[15]*

These are words I now live by. Obviously, I've grown as a result of my experience. I'm older, and I've mastered the fine art of flying like an eagle through calamities that I used to find so intimidating. I now define failure as one of the many lanes along the journey to victory. Ironically, I'm embracing a philosophy that a number of young people seem to understand very early in life.

* * *

Surviving the Shift

Unfortunately, millions of business owners around the United States experienced failure during the COVID-19 pandemic. According to a study by the Federal Reserve, an additional two hundred thousand businesses permanently closed during the first year of the pandemic, on top of the 600,000 establishments that typically shut down every year.[16] That's staggering when you think about it.

Losing your business because of circumstances beyond your control is nothing to be ashamed about. Because of changing social trends and, of course, the Internet's infinite pool of information, an increasingly healthy outlook about failure is taking root. I've met young people who are so naturally resilient, they don't seem to sweat it when the businesses they have dreamt about for years collapse on the first try. I applaud them. They have my utmost respect. And now, after nearly fifty years of entrepreneurial mountains and valleys, I, too, have a come-what-may point of view. I also have assorted gems that I have collected along the way.

I call them The Twelve Tenets of a Good Failure:

1. ***Don't be afraid of failure.*** *As J. K. Rowling says, "It is impossible to live without failing at something, unless you live so cautiously you might as well not have lived at all—in which case, you fail by default."[17]*

2. ***Do not quit.*** *"If you're going through hell, keep going,"*

216

Winston Churchill once admonished. He added, "Never give in, never give in, never, never, never, never—in nothing, great or small, large or petty!"[18]

3. **Do not wallow.** *Don't think "woe is me" or convince yourself that you're the only one in the world who has had this happen. There's a lot of company in this club. Mary Kay Ash quit her sales job after she was passed over for a promotion by a man she had trained. With a $5,000 investment, she launched her own direct-sales cosmetics company, which had $3 billion in revenue in 2020. She never wallowed in her circumstances. "For every failure, there's an alternative course of action," she said. "You just have to find it. When you come to a roadblock, take a detour."*[19]

4. **Apply what you learned from the experience.** *In Henry Ford's words, "Failure is simply the opportunity to begin again, this time more intelligently."*[20]

5. **Learn something from every adversity.** *Every mistake comes with a lesson.*

6. **Look for the blessing in your failure.** *What miracle or new opportunity does it contain? When Regal Plastics was failing, I became more concerned about my health. Someone put me in touch with Dr. Terry Gordon, and he's been my doctor, adviser, and friend ever since. I'm also far more conscious of diet and exercise than I was in the past.*

7. **Keep your eye on the prize.** *As you leapfrog out of the chaos and onward to greater heights, visualize what victory looks like. See yourself there!*

8. ***Maintain an attitude of gratitude.*** *Things went wrong. So what? Don't dwell on that. Be thankful for what is going right. The Leaning Tower of Pisa wasn't originally designed to lean. But guess what? If it stood straight, you probably would have never heard of it.*

9. ***Never lose your enthusiasm, your zest.*** *Rev. Martin Luther King Jr. said, "We must accept finite disappointment, but never lose infinite hope."[21]*

10. ***Find someone to talk to about your situation.*** *Don't allow embarrassment to prevent you from confiding in your friends.*

11. ***Do not wear your problems as a badge of courage.*** *But don't wear them as a mournful face either. Smile and stand tall.*

12. ***Do not blame everyone else.*** *Don't start blaming Black folks, white folks, your mama, or your friends. There's no honor in the blame game.*

My experiences have taught me that, every day, each and every one of us is either on the verge of failure or on the verge of success. We're either going through a crisis, coming out of a crisis, or approaching a crisis we don't know about yet. Hopefully, we won't get slapped in the face with another as big as the COVID-19 pandemic.

Regardless of what your crisis might be, when it happens, face it on your feet. You're going to have troubles. You're going to have money sometimes that you think is yours, then discover that, out of the $8 million you just made, the government is going to take $4 million. You might find out an associate is stealing from you. You might overreach like I did and watch what you have built swiftly fall apart.

It doesn't matter—*as long as you grow*. Adopt Oprah's attitude and think of it as a "moment in time."

"Go ahead, fall down," she says. "The world looks different from the ground."[22]

The billionaire Mark Cuban, owner of the Dallas Mavericks and star of the TV hit *Shark Tank*, knows all about falling down and getting back up. He opened a bar in college that was promptly closed down, he was fired from his first three jobs after graduating from Indiana University, then he tried to sell powdered milk, of all things. Flash forward to 1990, when he sold his start-up company, MicroSolutions, to CompuServe for $6 million, and nine years later unloaded Broadcast.com to Yahoo for $5.7 billion in stock.

"It doesn't matter how many times you [screw] up," Cuban said. "You only gotta be right once."[23]

In other words, chalk failures up to experience, then spread your wings wide. Accept that failure is inevitable. Own your mistake and be honest with yourself. Figure out why it happened and devise safeguards so that it doesn't happen again. Don't beat yourself up. Use failure as motivation and get back in the game. As Maya Angelou advised, "You may encounter many defeats, but you must not be defeated. It may even be necessary to encounter some defeats to know who you are."

"Who you are" is based on the label you are using for yourself. Are you labeling yourself a winner or a loser? You can't steal second base if you never get off first base. So how can you be a loser when you were heroic enough to take the dare? And how can you be a winner if you're not in the game, the competition, the race? Think long and hard about that question. And here's another one to consider: if a person sets a brand-new world record, he or she is considered first. But what about the old record that person just beat? If the old record of 9.78 seconds is broken by someone who ran 9.78 seconds, this doesn't mean the second place person broke the record too. Second place could have run 9.68 seconds; it's OK to have your record broken. That sounds pretty cool to me. I don't know how anyone could possibly describe it as a lesser accomplishment.

The only failure that ever occurs is the one an individual plasters on the walls of his or her own mind. I've always been taken aback by the idea that at one time Edwin "Buzz" Aldrin, one of the three American astronauts who made the original trip to the moon in 1969, put himself in this category. He even became an alcoholic. Neil Armstrong was the first man in the history of the world to set foot on the moon. Buzz Aldrin followed. The third astronaut, Michael Collins, hovered above the moon in a vessel dubbed the *Columbia*. Yet it's been said that Aldrin didn't take kindly to being second. He also felt sort of awkward because his step down onto the moon's rugged surface was less than graceful. He miscalculated the gravitational pull, didn't leap high enough, and missed a step by an inch. That near slip stirred up some moon dust, causing it to settle around the legs of his space suit. This was a minor embarrassment and a hint at possible imperfection. That's heavy, isn't it? He was literally walking on the moon and yet, at one point, thought of himself as not quite measuring up.

So my questions are: what determines whether someone has failed? On the flip side, what is the definition of success? What is the difference between "I failed" and "I'm a failure?" I mean, how does it look, and who makes that decision anyway? I think the answers lie somewhere in the punch line of an old sports joke.

A couple of players on a community baseball team were arguing furiously. One claimed the pitcher had thrown a ball and the other said, "You're crazy! That was a strike." They went back and forth, stamping their feet and loudly making their case. Suddenly, they heard a deep, gravelly voice. It was the umpire, and, man, was he irritated. He glared at both the men and growled, "It ain't nothing until I call it!"

I am that umpire. You are that umpire. Others may shout "loser," but that's their opinion. I make the calls in my life, and I don't see "out" as an option. And neither should you. *Starting* a business is tough. *Staying* in business is a whole lot tougher. But the beat goes on. That means you'll be just fine. All you have to do is remember one simple thing:

Failure is never fatal, and success is never final. Whether you win or lose, there's always next time.

CHAPTER 8

PRINCIPLE 7:
Cultivate Strong Faith

*Faith is taking the first step when
you don't see the whole staircase.*
—Rev. Martin Luther King Jr.

THE AROMA OF ripe Georgia peaches was wafting through the air, and the backyard swallows were chirping so loudly they might as well have joined the church choir. I sat up straight and tried to ignore the distractions. Dressed in my Sunday best, I was sitting in the cramped auditorium of Thomastown School and feeling kind of sweaty. It was early summer, and it was downright hot. But there was an amazing speaker standing on the stage, and despite my discomfort, he had my undivided attention.

I was graduating from eighth grade, and here was Otis

Moss, a student from the esteemed Morehouse College, giving the commencement address. I was much too young to grasp everything he was saying or to understand that Morehouse was only sixty miles away. But I was mesmerized by his words.

He said that every one of us—small-town kids from the red hills of Troup County—could grow up and be anything in the world. At first, I didn't believe him. But then again, he had to know what he was talking about. After all, he attended Morehouse, and to a kid growing up in LaGrange, Georgia, during the 1950s, meeting someone from Morehouse was like meeting an NBA player. In my neck of the woods, he was like a celebrity, and here he was, giving us a pep talk.

He told us to reach higher and higher. He said we were smart. We could achieve anything. He ended by saying that success would be ours, and when it happened, we must serve.

"If you have success with no service," he said, "you are worse than a thief and a robber."

I held on to his message. It became the kindling for the fire that would light my way and teach me the true meaning of faith. I began to realize that faith is not just the belief you hold in God; faith is how you *follow* that belief. It is your inspiration, the fuse you electrify when you create new goals and expand your dreams. It's the spark that pushes you to stay the course.

Faith was already a big part of my world back then. The fact is, it was my whole world. If you grew up in the South at that time, you were in a neighborhood, a parish, or an enclave where people told you constantly that you were special and that you were going to college. Once a month, our principal, Mr.

Griggs, would assemble all the little boys in a separate class-room. (The girls went elsewhere, and I have no idea what was said to them.) The boys were told we were going to Morehouse. In my case, Mr. Griggs would say I was going to graduate from Morehouse and become a preacher. I believed this for years.

All that changed when I turned fourteen and my family moved to Flint, Michigan. Suddenly, my confidence and funda-mental beliefs were shattered. In Flint, I had to try to adjust to an integrated school and classes that were a bit more advanced than my schoolwork in rural Georgia. For the first time in my life, I was competing with both Black and white students. Most of them were ahead of me academically and socially, and I got caught up in trying to prove myself. I guess I was plagued by the idea that I wasn't cool enough. My Southern diction wasn't big-city enough.

Instead of perceiving myself as smart, I saw myself as a country boy who stuttered occasionally and couldn't keep pace with his urban peers. Distracted by a new environment, I forgot all about Morehouse and the ideology that had been instilled in me for years.

It took quite a while, but eventually I began to pull together all the fractured pieces and rebuild my broken self-image. When I did, I discovered that the faith cultivated during my early years was still my core, the divine glue that held everything in my life together. I remembered what Dr. King famously said: "You ought to discover some principle, you ought to have some great faith that grips you so much that you will never give it up. Somehow you go on and say, 'I know that the God that I worship is able to deliver me, but if not, I'm going on anyhow, I'm going to stand up for it anyway!'"[1]

This realization turned out to be the most important aspect of my personal growth and the crux of my eventual success. When I jumped on the business scene in my late twenties, my partners and I had very little money. We worked hard, we partied "like it was 1999," and we all believed in God. That faith enabled us to knock on Wall Street's door and shoot for excellence. I feel it should be that way for every newbie.

YOU GOTTA HAVE FAITH IN SOMETHING

It's difficult to build a business without a formidable belief system. As an entrepreneur, you absolutely must have faith in something—faith when things are picture-perfect and faith when it all goes haywire.

Take FedEx founder Fred Smith, for instance. While he was still a student at Yale University, Smith had already devised his plan to revolutionize the package delivery industry. But when he wrote about it in a term paper, his professor scoffed at the idea and graded the assignment a measly C.

Smith wasn't swayed. In the early 1970s, he launched FedEx, the first company of its kind to rely on vans, airplanes, and posting stations to rush parcels to homes and businesses across the country overnight. The company took off like a rocket and then, suddenly, began to fizzle. A few months later, Smith found himself with a $24,000 fuel debt and only $5,000 in his company's bank account.

Now, this is where the situation gets tricky.

Smith had something known as *fervor.* He had audacity. He was filled with imagination, tenacity, and a quiet little passion called hope. Put them all together and they spell FAITH. The young entrepreneur flew to Las Vegas with his last $5,000 and gambled it all on the blackjack table. On Monday morning, he returned to his office with $27,000 in winnings—enough to pay the fuel bill and prevent his business from going bankrupt.

The lesson to be learned here is that there is nothing stronger or more amazing than the power of intention. When you intend to make something happen, your mind is made up, and a made-up mind has often been defined as one of the most potent forces in the universe. In the jargon of contemporary positive thinking, this means that where thought goes, a whole lot of energy flows. You become magnetized to your goal because you firmly believe in it.

You are demonstrating that unswerving faith defined by the Bible as the "substance of things hoped for, the evidence of things not seen" (Hebrews 11:1 KJV). When you're that convinced about something, it has to happen. Why? You're free of doubt. You have embraced the object of your desire and decreed it in the name of a power higher than yourself.

In my case, that higher power is God Almighty. I'm not knocking Smith. His actions, though unconventional, saved his business. But because faith in God is the backbone of my existence, I know for sure that I would not have placed my trust in Vegas. When problems are mounting, I take them to the cross. I spend time in prayer, calling on the God I know can fix anything.

However, faith is an individual thing, expressed in countless ways. Some tap into it by means of their own willpower and self-confidence while others turn to prayer, meditation, or religious services in a mosque, synagogue, temple, or church. Whatever your choice, you need the support of something greater than womankind and mankind—be it God, Allah, Jehovah, Yahweh, Buddha, or divine energy. When the cash flow is low and you're grasping at straws, sometimes the only thing you can do is seek out spiritual solace and hold on to the promise of grace.

George Shirley, the first Black tenor to sing a leading role with the Metropolitan Opera, is an exquisite example of this. Shirley, who once worked at a Detroit high school where he taught voice lessons to Motown artists Diana Ross, Smokey Robinson, and Mary Wilson, carved out a beautiful niche for himself in a profession that was not always kind to Black performers. I once had the honor of meeting Shirley, and he told me something that gave me chills. He said he succeeded against the odds because he had an abiding faith that was fueled by his link to those who had walked before him.

"My people were slaves," he said. "God placed within them a voice box for music and a seed and drive for music they could not fully express. And here I am more than one hundred years later with the genes, the physical structure, the lungs, and the opportunity to maximize this gift."

Shirley went on to say that his belief in God deepened

each time he sang, for every time he exercised his vocal cords, he was engaging in a sacred experience—bringing alive the pain, the beauty, and the faith of his African American ancestors.

As Maya Angelou so eloquently wrote in her poem "And Still I Rise," "I am the dream and the hope of the slave. I rise. I rise. I rise."[2] Faith is a highly personal form of rising to the occasion. It's a lofty moniker for a trust that tugs at each spirit and summons us to different missions. But for everyone, it serves the same purpose: To instill calmness in the midst of strife. To empower. To demonstrate the impossible. To create a profound connection to God.

Believe me, when you hit those financial potholes and the rubber meets the road, you have to find something to guide you. I happen to believe God always sends an angel, an interceptor, a message, a symbol. Sometimes you're so overwhelmed you can't see it, feel it, or hear it. That's when you have to get quiet and listen to that small voice within. As songwriter and gospel vocalist James Cleveland sings, "Peace be still."

Sometimes you just have to be still. Then you have to know in your heart that what you're requesting has already happened. As Mark 11:24 (NIV) states, "Therefore I tell you, whatever you ask for in prayer, believe that you have received it, and it will be yours."

FAITH IN ACTION

How can you tell whether you are truly living in faith? A pastor I know once explained it as knowledge from within that no one can erase. This pastor said he had a vision that his seven-year-old son would, one day, become a professional football player. To help his son train, he videotaped football games. Of course, like any fan, he saved the games that ended in a victory for his favorite team.

In one of his sermons, the pastor—whose son made it all the way to the NFL—compared his faith to the way he experiences a televised rerun of a sporting event. Although he knows how it's going to end, he reacts to every play. When a player fumbles the ball, he yells, "Oh, no!" When a player leaps in the air and catches a long one, he shouts, "Oh, yeah! That's what I'm talkin' about!"

He's aware of the winning team because the game was taped, and the outcome had already been revealed on ESPN and the six o'clock news. But he allows himself to move through a range of emotions and get the feel of the live game. He sees this practice as an analogy for everyday life.

"During my down times, I know God is going to deliver," he explained. "But I got to go through each stage—the ups, the downs, the sideways, the pushbacks, the setbacks. But I know how it's going to end."

This is the same approach that's been helpful for me. My deep-seated faith tells me that God is gathering all the pieces and patching them back together. Yet I still have to climb the hills and swim through the creeks. After Regal Plastics failed, there was no message louder and clearer than that. I had pulled through the debacle, gotten my emotions back on track, and even made a deal with a company that wanted to buy one of the plants. Then, at the last minute, the buyer pulled out and left me strapped with a $900,000 debt.

But my ordeal was over, and I knew it. In my heart, I was sure everything would be A-OK. As I made phone calls, reached out to my network, and followed the proper protocol, I was simply going through the motions like my pastor friend. All the while, I spoke like it was going to work out. I acted like I knew it was going to work out. I believed it was going to work out—and it did.

That's the best kind of faith—faith in action. In his book *Love, Medicine & Miracles*, Dr. Bernie Siegel writes, "When you suffer a misfortune, you are faced with the choice of what to do with it. You can wring good from it, or more pain."

He goes on to say, "Spirituality, unconditional love and the ability to see that pain and problems are opportunities for growth and redirection—these things allow us to make the best of the time we have . . . We see that there is no real past or future, and that as soon as we start thinking in terms of past and future, regretting, and wishing—we lose ourselves in judgmental thinking."[3]

Indeed, we have the power to change our lives, overcome hardships, and heal ourselves—through faith. Study after study shows heart patients recovering, cancer patients surviving, even crops growing better when they have been the target of ongoing prayer. Dr. Dale Matthews, a Maryland physician and author of *The Faith Factor*, analyzed more than two hundred studies linking faith to health. He says that prayer reduces the chance of illness and speeds recovery time for those who are healing from surgery and debilitating diseases.[4] Meanwhile, Dr. Harold Koenig of Duke University says prayer inhibits cortisol and other stress hormones that have a negative impact on the immune system.[5] By the same token, he believes faith floods the immune system with peace.

We're not talking barrels of faith. According to Scripture, you need less than a drop: "He replied, 'If you have faith as small as a mustard seed, you can say to this mulberry tree, 'Be uprooted and planted in the sea,' and it will obey you" (Luke 17:6 NIV). You only need the faith of a mustard seed.

On one of my many visits to Atlanta, I observed this firsthand. There was a news story on TV about an armed robbery at a restaurant. A reporter was interviewing the fearless woman whose quick thinking helped save the lives of the people who worked at a steakhouse she managed. When the news station played back the tape of her 911 call, I listened carefully and couldn't get over the peace in her voice. The reporter asked how she had remained so calm, and she replied that she owed it to her corporate training. Yet I knew better. She was walking by faith. I don't know what name she gave it or what had shaped her beliefs, but it was clear to me that she had stared fear in the eyes and handed over the control of that situation to something unseen.

I remember another event in Atlanta in which a woman put her faith in God to get her out of a harrowing encounter. Ashley Smith was a crystal meth addict who had lost custody of her daughter. But she was trying to turn her life around and was reading the Bible. On March 12, 2005, Brian Nichols, who was on trial for rape, overpowered a deputy and shot dead a judge, court reporter, and US customs agent. He escaped the courthouse and ended up at Smith's apartment. She didn't know him and was taken hostage. For seven hours, she shared her newly found faith in Christ. She suggested that maybe God had a plan for him to spread the gospel to other men in prison. Eventually, Nichols released her and surrendered to police peacefully. She quit using drugs and remarried.

"I haven't any plans to meet Brian in jail—it still feels too soon for that," she wrote in 2015. "But if I saw him, the first thing I'd do is thank him for allowing God to let him spare my life."[6]

We all have experienced it again and again. How many times during your college years has the book money run out, or your loans were maxed out, and you couldn't call home because you felt you would be a burden? And yet you made it through! Have you ever wondered where your next meal would come from and then, at the eleventh hour, someone stopped by your apartment or dorm room and ordered pizza? Remember, I once lived in a college dormitory that the other students called Hungry Hall. It didn't serve food, but my roommate never sweated it, and neither did I. We got by even though there were days when all we had was peanut butter, crackers, and—do I need to repeat it again? Faith. Faith. And more faith.

Faith is what inspired a little Black girl with polio to run track and try out for the Olympics. That girl, Wilma Rudolph, was a sickly child who had to wear a brace on her left leg. Through physical therapy and sheer determination, she conquered her disability and, in 1960, became a champion runner, the first African American woman to win three gold medals at a single Olympics.[7]

Faith is what convinced a young dreamer in the inner city of Dallas that he could hoop even though his height had peaked at five-foot-seven. Relying on speed and remarkable jumping ability, Anthony Jerome "Spud" Webb proved to his detractors that stature has nothing to do with skill. He played professionally and was noted for winning a slam-dunk contest despite being one of the shortest players in NBA history.[8]

Faith is what led a bedridden boy in Hoover, Alabama, to become one of the greatest coaches of all time. When young Bobby Bowden was stricken with rheumatic fever in 1943, he prayed to God to heal him. If God did, he promised, he would spend the rest of his life serving him. Coaching became Bowden's calling in life, and he guided Florida State University to two national championships and twenty-eight consecutive bowl games. More importantly, he taught hundreds of players how to be better men, husbands, and fathers. He took his players to church and boldly talked to them about faith. Even from his deathbed, Bowden relied on his steadfast faith. "I've always tried to serve God's purpose for my life, on and off the field, and I am prepared for what is to come," he said.[9]

Faith is what drove a young lady from a family of twelve to become owner of a restaurant that paid her to flip burgers as a teen. Her name is Deborah Virgiles, and she was one spunky, hardworking girl. When I met her, she was a sixteen-year-old student at Chadsey High School in Detroit. I hired her to work at my first McDonald's and watched in awe as she rose through the ranks. By the time I had acquired seven franchises, she had moved from the kitchen to the head of my human resources department. She was also ready to open her own franchises. Her first two flopped—one in a mall and another in a grocery store. But propelled by faith, she forged ahead and eventually ended up with several thriving McDonald's restaurants. Deborah, whom I am proud to call my mentee, became an American success story—from part-time employee to owner. That is the American Dream, is it not?

And is it not the essence of faith? I can say for a fact that Deborah radiated faith, though I can't claim to know where it comes from. Like Deborah, I feel it in every fiber of my being. But I'm not sure why some people have it and others don't. I have to assume that, for me, it's the result of attending a one-room church in Georgia, built and owned by my family. If you were a child back in my day, the elders who made you wash behind your ears and put on your Sunday-go-to-meeting clothes once a week were the people who instilled your faith.

All morning and much of the afternoon were spent in a pint-sized building filled with music, stomping, preaching, and joyous celebration. Mind you, if my parents had given me a choice, this would not have been the first thing on my to-do list. But I was accustomed to it and found some aspects pretty cool. Most Sundays, the men of the church handled the preaching and the women served on the usher board. But one Sunday a month was special because the traveling preacher would show up and deliver a fiery sermon. I still remember the big breakfasts of fried chicken, fish, biscuits, bacon, eggs, and gravy that my grandmother, Mammie Gordon, cooked on those days.

Then we'd all gather and pray. I now realize our prayers of "Lord, thank you for waking me up this morning" were creating the foundation for the gratitude and basic decency I live by today. I regard that foundation as my blueprint—not just for support during a crisis or as a means to acquire wealth, but as a way of thinking and being. When you open a franchise with three people and have little or no training, you've got to walk by something other than the McDonald's proven methodology. You need a philosophy on coping, giving, and treating people fairly.

Some of us are introduced to God much later in life. Chris Pratt, the star of *Jurassic World* and *Guardians of the Galaxy*, didn't become a Christian until he was nearly twenty years old when a man at a grocery store in Hawaii told him, "I stopped because Jesus told me to stop and talk to you." For some reason, Pratt listened to the stranger and accompanied him to church the next day. He stopped using drugs and became a devout Christian. That led him to his calling as an actor.[10]

Kurtis Walker, or Kurtis Blow, is widely recognized as the first commercially successful rapper of our time. His song "The Breaks" was the first certified gold record by a hip-hop artist, and he released fifteen albums. In 2009, Walker became an ordained minister and helped launch the Hip-Hop Church in Harlem to effectively deliver the good news to urban youth. The church vows to,

Deliver the same soul-saving, peace giving message of the loving Jesus Christ . . . [and to] reach out to the urban community, to the unchurched and de-churched; further exemplifying Jesus's consistently intentional acts of seeking reaching out and connecting to those who have traditionally been both economically and spiritually marginalized. Hip-Hop Church is available to people who want to meet God in a manner that relates to their lives, their music, and other elements of their lifestyle.[11]

Everyone has to figure out where they want to fit on the faith continuum. But I don't believe I would be where I am today if I had not been taught to adhere to these basic spiritual rules. Faith has sustained me. It has propped me up. When the doors were closed, it pointed me toward the windows. It has given me a sound moral compass that helped me adhere to the ideals that Morehouse student Otis Moss planted within me so many years ago. I realized God had a plan for me. As Oprah Winfrey said, "I believe every one of us is born with a purpose. No matter who you are, or how far you think you have to go, you have been tapped by a force greater than yourself to step into your God-given calling."[12]

I sincerely believe I have to treat people the way I want to be treated regardless of race, gender, and station in life. I learned at an early age to "do unto others as I would have others do unto me." In business, this can be accomplished at the level of management as fair hiring practices and deals that are carried out with integrity.

Or it can be practiced in very basic ways.

I remember one time an elderly man came into one of our McDonald's franchises and ordered a Filet-O-Fish sandwich with mustard. Instead, he was told it would be served with tartar sauce. At the time, that was one of McDonald's standard policies. He complained, but the young lady waiting on him refused to bend. After witnessing this interaction, I had an immediate flashback to the fish fries held at our church in LaGrange every Friday night. I remember vividly that we always slathered yellow mustard on the fish. So this particular evening I bent the rules a bit. Although my employee was following corporate guidelines, I didn't think we had the right to argue with a customer about what he should eat on *his* sandwich.

She kept saying no, and brotherman, who no doubt was from the South, kept demanding mustard. Without saying a word, I stepped behind the counter, got a courtesy cup, filled it with mustard and handed it to the gentleman. This was plain, old-fashioned common sense and an example of meeting people where they are. In business, as in life, treat people the way they want to be treated.

I didn't know a thing about karma back then, and I don't know much about it now. But I was taught that you reap what you sow, and it's something I will never stop believing. I don't know about most people, but I probably lean a little too much toward my original training. That has stuck with me since I began my career path as a social worker. I believe in blessing others. I also subscribe to a train of thought shared by activist Marian Wright Edelman, who wrote, "Service is the rent we pay for being. It is the very purpose of life and not something you do in your spare time."[13]

When I was much younger, I started worrying that I had not lived up to that ideal. It seemed to me that, perhaps, I could have done more as a social worker than an entrepreneur. Philanthropist and billionaire Richard DeVos, cofounder of Amway, is the one who turned on the light and woke me up. I was thirty and he was around fifty, and I told him how I felt. His answer was priceless.

"Wait a minute," he said. "How many people do you employ?"

"About seventy or seventy-five," I said.

"Well, that's the best social work in the world. You're providing jobs."

I had never thought about it like that. Yet I have no doubt in my mind that without my spiritual focus, I would have kept more money to myself and not be as fulfilled as I am today. Everyone has to decide how they want to give back or pay it forward. For some, it might be organizing a scuba diving club. Obviously, that's not Bill Pickard. For others, it might be mentoring a young man in calculus or teaching Sunday School.

There are various ways we can all serve. Some people donate time, some people write a check, and some can do both. Be grateful that you have the capacity to do either. No matter how successful you become, never forget to be supremely thankful for your blessings, and remember, "to whom much is given, much is required" (Luke 12:48, paraphrase). You have a responsibility to assist those who are less fortunate. As a man of faith, I see it as an obligation. Just do something nice for someone. You'll be surprised by how fulfilling it will be.

Not everyone agrees with me, but I also have the idealistic notion that *pathology* can be turned into *hopeology*. That's a term I coined to explain that lives can be transformed by scholarships, job training, and counseling. I've heard stories of at-risk youth whose attitudes did an about-face after meeting the right person, being exposed to an uplifting program, or landing a good opportunity. Without hope, there is no future.

* * *

Surviving the Shift

Undoubtedly, there were a lot of people questioning their faith as the world shut down during the COVID-19 pandemic. How could God allow a deadly virus to spread so rapidly around the world? How could God allow five million people to die? How could God allow millions of people to be out of work, leaving so many families struggling to come up with the money to put food on the table and pay their rent or mortgage?

But as I've mentioned, if you truly have faith, you simply stay the course and know that God has a plan, and that everything will work out in the end. It was comforting for me to know that far more people became stronger in their faith during the pandemic. A survey by Pew Research Center in April 2020 found that 24 percent of Americans said their religious faith grew during the pandemic, while only 2 percent said their faith became weaker. The same survey noted that Black Americans were twice as likely as whites to say their faith was stronger because of the pandemic.[14]

Like almost everything else, places of worship were closed during the pandemic because of social distancing requirements. Churches around the world moved their services to streaming channels so parishioners could access them virtually. That's how I found Dr. Frederick D. Haynes III, the senior pastor of Friendship-West Baptist Church in Dallas. Let me tell you something: he's one *bad man*. His fire-and-brimstone sermons might include everything from Elijah to 50 Cent. The man simply *brings it* every Sunday.

Haynes's family left the segregated South when he was a child and moved to San Francisco, where his grandfather and father, Frederick D. Haynes Jr., pastored churches. Tragedy struck Haynes when he was just fourteen. On the first day of school, his father suddenly died. In his grief, Haynes III strayed from God's path for him for a while, but he eventually found his way. He attended Bishop College in Dallas and Southwestern Baptist Theological Seminary. When he took over as senior pastor at Friendship-West Baptist Church in 1983, it had fewer than one hundred members. Today the church has more than twelve thousand members and has had to relocate three times to accommodate its growing congregation.

One of Haynes's favorite sayings is, "Shift happens." I guess it's the PG-13 version of the more popular catchphrase. During these troubling times, Haynes said he prayed more, read the Bible and inspirational books, and watched YouTube videos of his favorite preachers. When it seemed the world was crashing down on us, he wanted to get even closer to God. During a Zoom call with pastors in Florida, he told them, "Shepherds need to eat, too. And we have to find ways where we are fed so that we don't feel this emptiness."

During one particular sermon I watched, Haynes recounted the story of the abolitionist Harriet Tubman, who was known as the "Moses of her people." Historians believe she was born into slavery in Dorchester County, Maryland, and was enslaved until she and her two brothers escaped in 1849. Her husband, John, refused to leave with her. So after using the Underground Railroad to reach freedom in

Philadelphia, she went back to Maryland to get him. When she reached the plantation where he was enslaved, she called out for him. He didn't answer. She eventually learned that he hadn't waited on her and had married another woman, who was now pregnant.

"Shift happens, and every time that shift happens, you find yourself feeling like Harriet," Haynes said during the sermon. "[Tubman] cried out to God: 'God, you spoke to me. I did what you told me to do. Why did you bring me here to throw it up in my face? Why did you let me live?'"

Undeterred, Tubman returned to the South several times and helped dozens of slaves escape to freedom. She was so successful that slave owners put a $40,000 bounty on her head. She was never caught and never lost a passenger. She could have easily given up after learning about her husband.

"Life is filled with insufferable shifts of seasons, shifts that come out of nowhere," Haynes said. "Even when you decide to own your shifts, life will shift on you again."

The COVID-19 pandemic, like a tragic death, injury, financial troubles, divorce, or career change, is just another shift. Sure, it was a seismic shift that caused all of us to pause and reset for much longer than we wanted. But eventually, we'll come out on the other side, and things will begin to return to some level of normalcy.

Dr. Harold G. Koenig, a psychiatrist at Duke University, encouraged people to put their faith in action to maintain their health and well-being during the pandemic.[15] Here's what he recommended.

Deepen Your Religious Faith

Koening wrote that the pandemic is a wonderful time to grow closer to God through prayer; mediation; reading Scripture; listening to or watching inspirational programs on TV, podcasts, or the radio; and participating in virtual church services. Haynes talked about how God every now and then presses pause for our self-care. Maybe that's one of the silver linings of the pandemic.

"When life was 'normal,' one might have been so busy that there was no time for spiritual matters, with hobbies, jobs, housework, recreational activities, social and family activities filling up every moment of the day," Koenig wrote. "Now that normal activities have virtually come to a halt, there is lots of time for activities that will help build spiritual health."[16]

Haynes said he leaned on two Scriptures in particular. The first one is Matthew 11:28–30 (NIV):

Come to me, all you who are weary and burdened, and I will give you rest. Take my yoke upon you and learn from me, for I am gentle and humble in heart, and you will find rest for your souls. For my yoke is easy and my burden is light.

And the second is Philippians 4:6 (NIV):

Do not be anxious about anything, but in every situation, by prayer and petition, with thanksgiving, present your requests to God.

Haynes said he read those passages repeatedly during the pandemic to help with his mental health.

Love Thy Neighbor as Thyself

The Bible tells us we're supposed to love and care for our neighbors. I'm not talking about just the guy who lives next door or across the street. As Christians, we're supposed to help *anyone* in need. Be nice. Be kind. Be generous. People need help now more than ever before.

Use Technology

Could you imagine if the pandemic had hit before the age of the Internet and cell phones? People would have felt so isolated and alone. Thankfully, through Zoom, FaceTime, and other apps, we've been able to stay in touch with loved ones, friends, and work colleagues. Keep checking on others and make sure they're doing well. It means the world to them.

Pay Attention to Physical Health

Exercise. Sleep. Eat well. Take your vitamins. Drink plenty of water.

"Stay spiritually healthy, develop and nurture a close relationship with God, and volunteer to help family, friends, co-workers, and anyone else in need," Koenig wrote. "This will enhance physical health and resistance to infection, while spreading God's love to others."[17]

The Golden Key
to Success

My parting advice is that you keep ascending the ladder, and when you get to the top, reach back. Pathology dwells on the urban malaise of broken families, students performing below their grade level, and the cradle-to-grave prison pipeline. But the social worker who still resides in me doesn't feel the need to paint the entire predicament with one broad brushstroke. Young men and women with yearnings, talent, and potential can be found everywhere, and genius can emerge from the worst conditions.

I suppose this is the real reason I became an entrepreneur. The old joke is that an entrepreneur is someone who will work eighty hours a week for himself to avoid working forty hours a week for someone else. Maybe. But we also do it because we know that one day we will be in the position to pass on all that we have gained—and learned.

This is what I am doing now with this book. I've rounded up all my experiences and humbly placed them in your lap. What are you going to do with them? Will you shrug and say you're tired of people trying to give you directions? Or will you step out like I did? On faith.

The principle of faith is the culmination of all seven of my entrepreneurship principles. The vision and attitude you hold in your heart, the opportunities you seize, the finances you secure, the relationships you cultivate, the talent you hire, and the failure you transcend are all the result of your faith. Faith is the golden key, and with it everything else will lock itself into place.

Good luck! And remember, rivers get choppy and highways aren't always smooth, but no matter what stressors you encounter—high taxes, credit issues, defaulted loans—never lose sight of one fact: the banker you're dealing with might be a heck of a banker, but the God you serve is the CEO. Shift might happen, but remember that he is the one in control.

Acknowledgments

I'D LIKE TO EXTEND a special shout-out to the men of the Alpha Interest Groups as well as the Brothers of Alpha Phi Alpha Epsilon XI from Western Michigan University and the current and former team members of Global Automotive Alliance in several states and Canada.

I'd also like to thank the 1,000-plus young women and men who have worked at the McDonald's Bearwood Management Company for more than forty-five years and who, in essence, became our extended family.

Another special thank you goes to Denise Crittendon for working her magic and skillfully putting my ideas and experiences into words. In addition, I'm offering a heartfelt expression of gratitude to the many friends, associates, and editorial and marketing professionals who either lent a hand to this project or assisted me in other endeavors.

For your hard work, encouragement, and/or camaraderie: Reverend Charles G. Adams, Terry Alexander, David Allen,

Acknowledgments

Bill Allen, Don Allen, Charles Allen, William Ashburn, Pat Baker, Dean Percy Barnes, John Barth, Walter Beach III, Bob Beavers, Dean Le-Quita Booth, Melvin Bradley, Bob Brown, Maurene Brown-Smith, Bob Chappell, Paul Cheeks, Markita Choice, Roscoe Coleman, Robert C. Copeland, Donald Davis, Walter Davis, Richard DeVos Sr., Adam Doumbouya, Elaine Dowdell, DeWitt Dykes, Richard English, Mike Finney, Eddie Floyd, Diane Freeman, Doris Gamble, Thaddeus Garrett, Allan Gilmore, Benjamin Gordon, Dr. Conrad Graves, Trinita Grayson, Deborah Green-Virgiles, Stevie Green, William Griggs, Rita Haines, James Haines, Chuck Harvey, Angelo Henderson, Felicia Henderson, Sylvester Hester, Gail Hewitt, Ray Hirschman, Elliott Holland, Carol Hoover, Pat Hoover, Edgar B. Hope, Paul Hubbard Sr., Reverend Jesse L. Jackson, Harry E. Johnson, Jesse E. Johnson, Harold Johnson, Dr. Arthur L. Johnson, John H. Johnson, Carolyn Jones, Judge Damon L. Keith, John W. Kellogg, Jack Kemp, Reverend Dr. Gerald Kisner, Dr. Francis Albert Kornegay, Harold R. Kutner, Melvin Larsen, Petra Lewis, Sam Logan, Donald Lubbers, John Mack, Phil Meek, Terri Moon, Rev. Otis Moss, Sr., James Nichols, Roger Penske, Revered Dr. James C. Perkins, Judson Pickard, Francis Pierce, Arnold Pinkney, Betty Pinkney, Arnold R. Pinkney, Anita Polk, John Popercheck, John Potts, James Randall, Nelly R. Reid, Dr. Marlo Rencher, R.O. Ridgeway, Harry Roberson, James Robinson, Ray Rogal, Dr. Albert Rogers, Lawrence Root, John Sagan, Alvin Schwartz, Dawn Scott-Batts, Pete Short, Martha Jean "The Queen" Steinberg, Frank Stellar, Charlie

Acknowledgments

Strong, Arthur Teele, Greg Trombley, Mary Turner, Abraham Venable, W.O. Walker, Herb Washington, Donald Westley, Bridget Williams, Leroy Woodyard, Robert L. Wright, Bryan Young, and Roger Young—I thank you.

Notes

Chapter 2: Develop Positive Vision and Attitude

1. Azim Jamal, "Internalizing Success," *The Citizen*, August 10, 2021, https://www.thecitizen.co.tz/tanzania/oped/-internalizing-success-3503770.

2. Steve Harvey, "Make a Vision Board," YouTube, November 26, 2018, https://www.youtube.com/watch?v=_LBJdqTYj24.

3. "Oprah's Obama Inauguration Dress Plan: It's All about the 'Vision Boards,'" *People*, November 4, 2008, https://people.com/style/oprahs-obama-inauguration-dress-plan-its-all-about-the-vision-boards/.

4. "Oprah's Obama Inauguration Dress Plan."

5. Adam Sicinski, "My Conversation with Albert Einstein about Creativity, Intuition and the Power of Curiosity," IQ Matrix (blog), https://blog.iqmatrix.com/albert-einstein#:~:text=Einstein%3A%20Without%20a%20doubt%20in,Imagination%20is%20in%20fact%20everything.&text=Einstein%3A%20Yes%2C%20of%20course.

6. Anna Williams, "8 Successful People Who Use the Power of Visualization," mind-bodygreen, July 8, 2015, https://www.mindbodygreen.com/ 0-20630/8-successful-people-who-use-the-power-of-visualization.html.

7. Rose Leadem, "Borrow Tom Brady's Trick for Visualizing a Super Bowl Success," *Entrepreneur*, January 31, 2017, https://www.entrepreneur.com/article/288552.

8. Richard Milner, "How Stephen King's First Bestseller Almost Ended Up in the Trash," Grunge, December 16, 2020, https://www.grunge.com/296865/how-stephen-kings-first-bestseller-almost-ended-up-in-the-trash/.

9. Eleanor Harvie, "15 Celebrities Whose Failures Led to Success," 15-celebrities-whose-failures-led-to-success/.

10. Stedman Graham and Stephen R. Covey, *You Can Make It Happen: A Nine-Step Plan for Success* (New York: Simon & Schuster, 1998), 11.

11. Phoebe Dampare Osei, "Saving: Where to Start and How You Can Save as Much as Possible," Yahoo! News, June 29, 2021, https://news.yahoo.com/saving-money-where-start-much-possible-100239689.html.

12. Kris Frieswick, "These Founders Hit the Road—and Found Their Next Big Idea," *Inc.*, November 6, 2017, https://www.inc.com/magazine/ 201711/ kris-frieswick/companies-inspired-by-travel.html.

13. "Lyft Net Worth 2017–2021: Lyft," Macrotrends, accessed August 25, 2021, https://www.macrotrends.net/stocks/charts/LYFT/lyft/net-worth#:~:text=Lyft%20net%20worth%20as%20of%20August%2023%2C%20 2021%20is%20%2415.84B.&text=Lyft%2C%20Inc.%20is%20a%20 ride,in%20the%20US%20and%20Canada.

14. Karen Gilchrist, "How Richard Branson Started Virgin Atlantic with a Blackboard Selling $39 Flights," CNBC, December 29, 2019, https://www.cnbc.com/2019/12/30/richard-branson-started-virgin-atlantic-with-a-board-and-39-flights.html.

15. "Nielsen's 2021 African American Consumer Report Explores the Influence of Black Culture on Content and Media Trends and the Representation of the Collective Black Community," Nielsen, October 26, 2021, https://ir.nielsen.com/ news-events/press-releases/news-details/2021/Nielsens-2021-African-American-Consumer-Report-Explores-the-Influence-of-Black-Culture-on-Content-and-Media-Trends-and-the-Representation-of-the-Collective-Black-Community/ default.aspx.

16. Paula Adams, *Rhythm: Uplifting Quotes from the African American Perspective* (New York: Balboa Press, 2020), 98.

17. Rachael Knodel, The Pensieve (blog), February 4, 2013, https://sites.psu.edu/ potterheadsforlife/2013/02/04/death-is-but- the-next-great-adventure/.

18. "Stress and Decision-Making during the Pandemic," American Psychological Association, accessed January 31, 2022, https://www.apa.org/news/press/ releases/stress/2021/october-decision-making.

19. "Stress and Decision-Making during the Pandemic."

20. Elizabeth Chuck, "Stress from the Pandemic Has Made Even Basic Decision-Making Difficult, Poll Finds," NBC News, October 27, 2021, https://www.

nbcnews.com/news/us-news/stress-pandemic-made-even-basic-decision-making-difficult-poll-finds-rcna3703.

21. "The Impact of Covid-19 on the Mental Health of Adolescents and Youth," UNICEF, October 4, 2021, https://www.unicef.org/lac/en/impact-covid-19-mental-health-adolescents-and-youth.

22. "Impact of Covid-19 on the Mental Health of Adolescents and Youth."

23. Leonard Cohen, "Anthem," track 5 on *The Future*, Columbia, 1992.

Chapter 3: Principle 2: Be Mindful of Opportunity

1. DeNeen L. Brown, "'Life or Death for Black Travelers': How Fear Led to 'The Negro Motorist Green-Book,'" *The Washington Post*, June 1, 2017, https://www.washingtonpost.com/news/retropolis/wp/2017/06/01/life-or-death-for-black-travelers-how-fear-led-to-the-negro-motorist-green-book/.

2. Jessica Millis, "10 Famous Companies That Were Founded by College Students," Lifehack, June 29, 2015, https://www.lifehack.org/articles/productivity/10-famous-companies-that-were-founded-college-students.html.

3. Rajat Bhageria, "An Interview with Seth Berkowitz: How the Founder of Insomnia Has Revolutionized the College Experience Armed Only with Cookies," *Huffington Post*, December 6, 2017, https://www.huffpost.com/entry/an-interview-with-seth-be_b_6638500.

4. "Uber Announces Results for Second Quarter 2021," Uber Technologies, accessed September 8, 2021, https://investor.uber.com/news-events/news/press-release-details/2021/Uber-Announces-Results-for-Second-Quarter-2021/default.aspx.

5. "About Us," Airbnb Newsroom, August 30, 2021, https://news.airbnb.com/about-us/.

6. Tricia McKinnon, "Why Doordash & Other Delivery Apps Struggle with Profitability," Indigo9 Digital, March 16, 2021, https://www.indigo9digital.com/blog/fooddeliveryappprofitability#:~:text=DoorDash's%20revenues%20in%20fourth%20quarter,224%25%20to%20reach%20%241.4%20billion.&text=Similarly%20DoorDash%20has%20never%20generated,a%20profit%20of%20%2423%20million.

7. Sean Ludwig, "10 Hugely Successful Companies That Reinvented Their Business," US Chamber of Commerce, December 4, 2020, https://www.uschamber.com/co/good-company/growth-studio/successful-companies-that-reinvented-their-business.

8. James Brown, "I Don't Want Nobody to Give Me Nothing (Open Up the Door, I'll Get It Myself)," King Records, 1969.

9. "Class of 2023: Final Class Profile," NYU Stern, accessed September 10, 2021, https://www.stern.nyu.edu/programs-admissions/full-time-mba/community/class-profile.

10. "NBA Foundation Priorities," NBA Foundation, December 11, 2020, https://nbafoundation.nba.com/priorities/.

11. Lolly Daskal, "7 Powerful Beliefs That Will Lead You to Success," *Inc.*, April 7, 2016, https://www.inc.com/lolly-daskal/7-powerful-beliefs-that-lead-to-monumental-success.html.

12. Susan Lund et al., "What's Next for Consumers, Workers, and Companies in the Post-Covid-19 Recovery," McKinsey & Company, May 18, 2021, https://www.mckinsey.com/featured-insights/future-of-work/whats-next-for-consuers- workers-and-companies-in-the-post-covid-19-recovery.

13. Lund et al., "What's Next for Consumers."

14. Robert Fairlie, "The Impact of Covid-19 on Small Business Owners: Evidence of Early-Stage Losses from the April 2020 Current Population Survey," SIEPR, May 1, 2020, https://siepr.stanford.edu/research/publications/impact-covid-19-small-business-owners-evidence-early-stage-losses-april-2020.

15. Quoctrung Bui, "Small Businesses Have Surged in Black Communities. Was It the Stimulus?," *The New York Times*, May 24, 2021, https://www.nytimes.com/2021/05/24/upshot/stimulus-covid-startups-increase.html.

16. Kim Wallace Carlson, "With Greater Access, More Black Entrepreneurs Would Thrive," Ewing Marion Kauffman Foundation, April 6, 2021, https://www.kauffman.org/currents/with-greater-access-more-black-entrepreneurs-would-thrive/#:~:text=Recently%2C%20the%20Kauffman%20Foundation%20convened,will%20be%20able%20to%20prosper.

17. Bui, "Small Businesses Have Surged."

18. Jordan Valinsky, "Peloton Sales Surge 172% as Pandemic Bolsters Home Fitness Industry," CNN Business, September 11, 2020, https://www.cnn.com/2020/09/11/business/peloton-stock-earnings/index.html.

19. Valinsky, "Peloton Sales Surge 172%."

20. Marie E. Saint-Cyr, personal correspondence with the author, April 4, 2021.

21. Marie E. Saint-Cyr, personal correspondence with the author, April 4, 2021.

22. Pat Franklin, "Down the Drain," Container Recycling Institute, May 27, 2020, https://www.container-recycling.org/index.php/issues/.../275-down-the-drain.

23. David M. Walker, personal correspondence with the author, April 29, 2021.

24. Debbie Phillips-Donaldson, "New Us Pet Ownership Study Confirms Pandemic-Led Growth," PetfoodIndustry.com RSS, June 1, 2021, https://www.petfoodindustry.com/articles/10325-new-us-pet-ownership-study-confirms-pandemic-led-growth.

25. Sarah McBride, "All Those Pandemic Puppies Mean Business for Dog-Walking Apps," *Bloomberg,* March 31, 2021, https://www.bloomberg.com/news/articles/2021-03-31/pandemic-pet-owners-turn-to-wag-rover-dog-walking-apps-as-normalcy-returns.

26. Corey Ackerman, personal correspondence with the author, June 30, 2021.

27. Corey Ackerman, personal correspondence with the author, June 30, 2021.

28. Caitlin Pyle, *Work at Home: The No-Nonsense Guide to Avoiding Scams and Generating Real Income from Anywhere* (New York: Ingram Publishing Services, 2019), 181.

29. Bui, "Small Businesses Have Surged."

30. Don Lee, "The Pandemic Saw a Boom in New Black-Owned Businesses—the Largest Surge in the Last Quarter-Century," *Los Angeles Times,* June 28, 2021, https://www.latimes.com/politics/story/2021-06-28/pandemic-silver-lining-black-owned-business-startups-surge-to-25-year-high.

Chapter 4: Principle 3: Look for Finance Options Everywhere

1. Kendrick Lamar, "Money Trees," track 5 on *Good Kid, M.A.A.D. City,* 2012.

2. Big Worm, "Friday," YouTube, May 7, 2008, https://www.youtube.com/watch?v=8hBg80CZMJ4.

3. Minda Zetlin, "If You're like One-Third of Americans, You Considered Starting a Business but Didn't Do It. Here's Why Not," *Inc.,* August 15, 2018, https://www.inc.com/minda-zetlin/starting-a-business-entrepreneurs-entrepreneurship-reasons-for-not-starting-a-business-capital-loans.html.

4. Sonari Glinton, "Esther Gordy Edwards, the Woman behind Motown," NPR, August 26, 2011, https://www.npr.org/sections/therecord/2011/08/26/139969371/esther-gordy-edwards-the-woman-behind-motown.

5. Laurel Wamsley, "Historic Black Church Donates $100,000 to Pay Off Debts of Howard U. Students," NPR, February 12, 2019, https://www.npr.org/2019/02/12/693953771/historic-black-church-donates-100-000-to-pay-off-debts-of-howard-u-students.

6. "Building Community Together" Local Investing Opportunities Network, accessed January 31, 2022, https://www.jeffersonlion.net/.

7. Earll Murman, "Lion Investments Top $10 Million in Our Area: Letter to the Editor," *Port Townsend Leader*, April 7, 2021, https://www.ptleader.com/stories/lion-investments-top-10-million-in-our-area-letter-to-the-editor,74539.

8. "Campaign Launches to Strengthen 1,000 Black-Owned Businesses in Atlanta," The Annie E. Casey Foundation, May 3, 2021, https://www.aecf.org/blog/campaign-launches-to-strengthen-1000-black-owned-businesses-in-atlanta.

9. Trevor Wheelwright, "How Much Americans Spend on Internet, Streaming, and Cell Phone Bills," Reviews.org, January 11, 2021, https://www.reviews.org/internet-service/cost-of-internet-streaming-and-cell-phone-bills/.

10. Ben Walker, "9 Simple Pieces of Advice from Jay-Z That Any Investor Can Use," FinanceBuzz, May 26, 2021, https://financebuzz.com/investing-advice-from-jay-z.

11. "2019 Modern Wealth Survey," Charles Schwab, https://www.aboutschwab.com/modernwealth2019.

12. "Despite Concerns about Being out of Work, Americans Increase Spending to Stockpile Goods," NORC at the University of Chicago, March 24, 2020, https://www.norc.org/NewsEventsPublications/PressReleases/Pages/despite-concerns-about-being-out-of-work-americans-increase-spending-to-stockpile-goods.aspx.

13. Fairlie, "Impact of Covid-19 on Small Business Owners."

14. Claire Kramer Mills and Jessica Battisto, "Double Jeopardy: Covid-19's Concentrated Health and Wealth Effects in Black Communities," Federal Reserve of New York, August 2020, https://www.newyorkfed.org/medialibrary/media/smallbusiness/DoubleJeopardy_COVID19andBlackOwnedBusinesses.

15. Mills and Battisto, "Double Jeopardy."

16. Kim Wallace Carlson, "With Greater Access, More Black Entrepreneurs Would Thrive," Ewing Marion Kauffman Foundation, April 6, 2021, https://www.kauffman.org/currents/with-greater-access-more-black-entrepreneurs-would-thrive/#:~:text=Recently%2C%20the%20Kauffman%20Foundation%20convened,will%20be%20able%20to%20prosper.

17. David M. Walker, personal correspondence with the author, April 29, 2021.

18. Anne Sraders, "Black-Owned Small Businesses Face Hurdles Even as COVID Eases and Optimism Rises," *Fortune*, June 18, 2021, https://fortune.com/2021/06/18/black-owned-small-businesses-obstacles-inequity-post-covid-recovery-small-business/.

19. Sraders, "Black-Owned Small Businesses Face Hurdles."

20. "Goldman Sachs *One Million Black Women* Announces Latest Round of Investments, Partnerships and Grants to Kick Off 2022," Goldman Sachs, accessed January 31, 2022, https://www.goldmansachs.com/media-relations/press-releases/2022/ombw-announces-latest-round-of-investments-partnership-and-grants-2022.html.

21. Anthony Ha, "Diversity-focused Harlem Capital Raises $134M," TechCrunch+, March 31, 2021, https://techcrunch.com/2021/03/31/harlem-capital-fund-ii/.

22. You can learn more about Harlem Capital's amazing work at https://harlem.capital.

23. Matt Kempner, "Zaxby's Co-Founder Sold His Drums to Start Chicken Chain," *The Atlanta Journal-Constitution*, April 11, 2014, https://www.ajc.com/business/zaxby-founder-sold-his-drums-start-chicken-chain/DeuLE5Cy6BM73KucS8yRcI/.

Chapter 5: Principle 4: Build Good Relationships

1. Dr. Dre, featuring Eminem, and Skylar Grey, "I Need a Doctor," 2011.

2. Dale Carnegie, *How to Win Friends and Influence People* (New York: Simon & Schuster, 2022).

3. "79% of Businesses Have Rejected a Job Candidate Based on Social Media Content; Job Seekers Should Post Online Carefully," Cision, April 28, 2020, https://www.prnewswire.com/news-releases/79-of-businesses-have-rejected-a-job-candidate-based-on-social-media-content-job-seekers-should-post-online-carefully-301048157.html.

4. "About Us," LinkedIn Pressroom, accessed January 31, 2022, https://news.linkedin.com/about-us#Statistics.

5. "LinkedIn Business Highlights from Microsoft's FY21 Q4 Earnings," July 28, 2021, https://news.linkedin.com/2021/july/

linkedin-business-highlights-from-microsoft-s-fy21-q4-earnings#:~:text=Included%20in%20the%20report%20on,first%20time%2C%20up%20 27%25.&text=LinkedIn%20has%20more%20than%20774,compared%20 to%20a%20year%20ago.

6. Susan Caminiti, "Here's How Zoom Is Helping Create the New World of Hybrid Work," CNBC, July 15, 2021, https://www.cnbc.com/2021/07/15/ heres-how-zoom-is-creating-the-new-world-of-hybrid-work-.html.

Chapter 6: Principle 5: Choose a Team with the Right Talent and Skill Set

1. A. H. Maslow, "A Theory of Human Motivation," *Psychological Review* 50, no. 4 (1943): 370–96, https://doi.org/10.1037/h0054346.

2. Jessica Durando, "15 of Nelson Mandela's Best Quotes," *USA Today*, December 6, 2013, https://www.usatoday.com/story/news/nation-now/2013/12/05/ nelson-mandela-quotes/3775255/.

3. Amelia Lucas, "Drive-thru Ordering Surged during the Pandemic. Fast-Food Chains Don't Think It's a Fad," CNBC, March 12, 2021, https://www.cnbc. com/2021/03/12/drive-thru-ordering-surged-during-the-pandemic-heres-what-comes-next.html.

4. John C. Maxwell, *150 Essential Insights on Leadership* (New York: Harvest House, 2021).

5. Amanda Stansell, "Highest Rated CEOS during the COVID-19 Crisis," Glassdoor, September 16, 2020, https://www.glassdoor.com/research/ highest-rated-ceos-coronavirus/.

6. Raisa Bruner, "Young People Are Leaving Their Jobs in Record Numbers—and Not Going Back," *TIME*, October 29, 2021, https://time.com/6111245/ young-workers-quitting/.

7. Bruner, "Young People Are Leaving."

8. Joyce Meyer, "Wait Patiently," Joyce Meyer Ministries, March 5, 2019, https:// joycemeyer.org/dailydevo/2019/03/0305-wait-patiently.

9. Emily Barone, "The Pandemic Forced Thousands of Businesses to Close—but New Ones Are Launching at Breakneck Speed," *TIME*, July 22, 2021, https:// time.com/6082576/pandemic-new-businesses/.

Chapter 7: Principle 6: Do Not Overreact to Failure

1. "Small Business Facts," Small Business Administration, June 2012, https://www.sba.gov/sites/default/files/Business-Survival.pdf?mod=article_inline.

2. Samra Khawaja, "Life according to F. Scott Fitzgerald," National Endowment for the Arts, September 20, 2016, https://www.arts.gov/stories/blog/2016/life-according-f-scott-fitzgerald.

3. Ronald Beghetto, *Big Wins, Small Steps: How to Lead for and with Creativity* (Thousand Oaks, CA: Corwin, 2016), 17.

4. Erica R. Hendry, "7 Epic Fails Brought to You by the Genius Mind of Thomas Edison," *Smithsonian*, November 20, 2013, https://www.smithsonianmag.com/innovation/7-epic-fails-brought-to-you-by-the-genius-mind-of-thomas-edison-180947786/.

5. Carolyn M. Brown, "Tyler Perry on How to Find Success after Failure," Black Enterprise, November 25, 2017, https://www.blackenterprise.com/tyler-perry-on-finding-success-after-failure/.

6. "Walt Disney," *Fortune*, August 3, 2021, https://fortune.com/company/disney/fortune500/.

7. "Actor Sidney Poitier: Striving for a Life of Excellence," Texas Public Radio, May 19, 2009, https://www.tpr.org/2009-05-19/actor-sidney-poitier-striving-for-a-life-of-excellence.

8. Elisabeth Brier, "Meet the Jackie Robinson of Wall Street," *Forbes*, April 3, 2021, https://www.forbes.com/sites/elisabethbrier/2021/04/03/reginald-f-lewis-jackie-robinson-of-wall-street-beatrice-lbo/?sh=3af1328c631d.

9. "Domino's Pizza® Announces Second Quarter 2021 Financial Results," Domino's Pizza, July 22, 2021, https://ir.dominos.com/news-releases/news-release-details/dominos-pizzar-announces-second-quarter-2021-financial-results.

10. "Make Your Own Circumstances," Proctor Gallagher Institute, accessed October 22, 2021, https://www.proctorgallagherinstitute.com/51120/make-your-own-circumstances.

11. Michael Jordan, "Thoughts on the Business of Life," *Forbes*, https://www.forbes.com/quotes/11194/.

12. T. J. Allan, "How Michael Jordan's Mindset Made Him a Great Competitor," USA Basketball, November 24, 2015, https://www.usab.com/youth/news/2012/08/how-michael-jordans-mindset-made-him-great.aspx.

13. Emily Temple, "The Most-Rejected Books of All Time (Of the Ones That Were Eventually Published)," Literary Hub, December 22, 2017, https://lithub.

com/the-most-rejected-books-of-all-time/#:~:text=%E2%80%9CIf%20
we%20had%20given%20up,of%20Motorcycle%20Maintenance%3A%20
121%20rejections.

14. Bryan E. Robinson, "Why Failure Is Your Ally," *Psychology Today*, September 18, 2020, https://www.psychologytoday.com/us/blog/the-right-mindset/202009/why-failure-is-your-ally; Ruth Simon, "Covid-19's Toll on U.S. Business? 200,000 Extra Closures in Pandemic's First Year," *The Wall Street Journal*, April 16, 2021, https://www.wsj.com/articles/covid-19s-toll-on-u-s-business-200-000-extra-closures-in-pandemics-first-year-11618580619.

15. Napoleon Hill, *Think & Grow Rich* (Shippensburg, PA: Sound Wisdom, 2010).

16. Ayelet Sheffy, "The Pandemic May Have Caused 200,000 Business Closures—Fewer Thank Expected," *Business Insider*, April 16, 2021, https://www.businessinsider. com/ small-business-closures-pandemic-less-expeced-past-year-fed-survey-2021-4.

17. J. K. Rowling, "Harvard Commencement Address," J. K. Rowling, accessed January 15, 2020, https://www.jkrowling.com/harvard-commencement-address/.

18. Winston Churchill, "Never Give In, Never, Never, Never, 1941," America's National Churchill Museum, https://www.nationalchurchillmuseum.org/never-give-in-never-never-never.html.

19. Karol Ladd, *The Power of a Positive Woman: Devotional & Journal* (New York: Howard Books, 2007), 98.

20. Erika Andersen, "21 Quotes from Henry Ford on Business, Leadership and Life," *Forbes*, accessed December 10, 2021, https://www.forbes.com/sites/erikaandersen/2013/05/31/21-quotes-from-henry-ford-on-business-leadership-and-life/?sh=473d35c9293c.

21. Holly Lebowitz Rossi, "Martin Luther King, Jr. on 'Infinite Hope,'" *Guideposts*, accessed January 14, 2022, https://www.guideposts.org/inspiration/inspiring-stories/stories-of-hope/martin-luther-king-jr-on-infinite-hope.

22. Melanie Curtin, "25 Oprah Winfrey Quotes That Will Empower You (and Make You Laugh)," *Inc.*, February 11, 2019, https://www.inc.com/melanie-curtin/25-oprah-winfrey-quotes-that-will-empower-you-and-make-you-laugh.html.

23. Taylor Locke, "3 Times Mark Cuban Failed before Becoming a Billionaire: 'You Only Gotta Be Right Once,'" CNBC, February 11, 2020, https://www.cnbc.com/2020/02/11/times-mark-cuban-failed-before-becoming-a-billionaire.html.

Chapter 8: Principle 7: Cultivate Strong Faith

1. "'In That Land of Perfect Day': Photographer Documents Life in the Delta," *Daily Leader*, August 2, 2019, https://www.dailyleader.com/2019/08/02/in-that-land-of-perfect-day-photographer-documents-life-in-the-delta/.

2. Sara Kettler, "Maya Angelou: The Meaning Behind Her Poem 'Still I Rise,'" *Biography*, January 29, 2021, https://www.biography.com/news/maya-angelou-still-i-rise.

3. Bernie S. Siegel, *Love, Medicine & Miracles: Lessons Learned About Self-Healing from a Surgeon's Experience with Exceptional Patients* (New York: William Morrow, 2015).

4. Dale A. Matthews and Connie Clark, *Faith Factor: Proof of the Healing Power of Prayer* (New York: Penguin, 1999).

5. "What Religion Can Do for Your Health," Beliefnet, https://www.beliefnet.com/wellness/health/2006/05/what-religion-can-do-for-your-health.aspx.

6. Jane Ridley, "I Was Taken Hostage—and It Saved My Life," *New York Post*, September 11, 2015, https://nypost.com/2015/09/11/how-being-held-hostage-by-a-crazed-gunman-saved-my-life/.

7. M. B. Roberts, "Rudolph Ran and World Went Wild," ESPN, http://www.espn.com/sportscentury/features/00016444.html.

8. Rhiannon Walker, "The Day Spud Webb Took Flight at the Slam Dunk Contest," Andscape, February 7, 2018, https://theundefeated.com/features/the-day-spud-webb-took-flight-at-the-slam-dunk-contest/.

9. "Longtime Florida State Football Coach Bobby Bowden Dies at 91," ESPN, August 8, 2021, https://www.espn.com/college-football/story/_/id/31986091/long-florida-state-football-coach-bobby-bowden-dies-91.

10. Laura Turner, "The Rise of the Star-Studded, Instagram-Friendly Evangelical Church," *Vox*, February 6, 2019, https://www.vox.com/culture/2019/2/6/18205355/church-chris-pratt-justin-bieber-zoe-hillsong.

11. "Kurtis Blow and Greater Hood Church Relaunch Hip-Hop Church," PR.com, March 8, 2019, https://www.pr.com/press-release/779171.

12. Brie Schwartz, "In Oprah's New Book, *The Path Made Clear*, She Shares Her Greatest Life Lesson Yet," Oprah Daily, November 2, 2021, https://www.oprahdaily.com/life/a26930708/oprah-path-made-clear/.

13. Max Wyn, "Marian Wright Edelman Delivers Stirring Speech," UCLA Luskin School of Public Affairs, December 6, 2013, https://luskin.ucla.edu/marian-wright-edelman-delivers-stirring-speech.

14. Claire Gecewicz, "Few Americans Say Their House of Worship Is Open, but a Quarter Say Their Faith Has Grown amid Pandemic," Pew Research Center, April 30, 2020, https://www.pewresearch.org/fact-tank/2020/04/30/few-americans-say-their-house-of-worship-is-open-but-a-quarter-say-their-religious-faith-has-grown-amid-pandemic/.

15. Harold G. Koenig, "Maintaining Health and Well-Being by Putting Faith into Action during the COVID-19 Pandemic," *Journal of Religion and Health* 59, no. 5 (October 2020): 2205–14.

16. Koenig, "Maintaining Health and Well-Being."

17. Koenig, "Maintaining Health and Well-Being."

About the Author

WILLIAM F. PICKARD, PH.D. is founder and executive chairman of Global Automotive Alliance (GAA), GAA New Ventures, comanaging partner at MGM Grand Detroit Casino, CEO of Bearwood Management, and co-owner of five Black-owned newspapers : *The Pittsburgh Courier, The Chicago Defender, The Atlanta Daily World,* and *The Michigan Chronicle.* All have evolved into Real Times Media, a media marketing company. (The *Memphis Tri-State Defender* is no longer part of the Black Newspaper ownership.).

Pickard's fifty-year entrepreneurial career began as a McDonald's franchisee. Since its founding in 1989, GAA has generated more than five billion dollars in sales with eight plants in the US and Canada, servicing corporations such as Boeing, Mercedes-Benz, General Motors, Delphi, Johnson Controls, Starbucks, The Home Depot, and Merck & Co. pharmaceuticals.

He is a philanthropist, supporting education at colleges and universities, including Western Michigan University, The Ohio State University, Florida A&M University, Spelman College, Clark Atlanta University, Morehouse College, and others.

ABOUT THE AUTHOR

Among his honors are the Morehouse College 34th Candle in the Dark Award for Entrepreneurship and Philanthropy, the Michigan Lifetime Humanitarian Award, and the Michiganians of the Year Award for his business success, civic leadership, and philanthropy.

Dr. Pickard holds a bachelor's degree from Western Michigan University, a master's degree from the University of Michigan, and a Ph.D. from The Ohio State University.